Picture Chinese
Art as Language

Sukming Lo

LONG RIVER PRESS

Published in the United States of America by

Long River Press

360 Swift Avenue, Suite 48

South San Francisco, CA 94080

www.longriverpress.com

Library of Congress Cataloging-in-Publication Data

Lo, Sukming.
 Picture Chinese: Art as Language =[Zhongguo wen zi] / Sukming Lo.
   p. cm.
 Parallel title in Chinese characters.
 Includes bibliographical references.
 ISBN 1-59265-069-4 (pbk.)
 1. Chinese characters—Study and teaching. I. Title. II. Title:
Art as Language. III. Title: Zhongguo wen zi.
PL1171.L545 2006
495.182'421—dc22
                                    2006040828

ISBN-10: 1-59265-069-4
ISBN-13: 978-1-59265-069-9
Printed in China

10 9 8 7 6 5 4 3 2 1

First Edition

For my parents,
and my daughter.

Table of Contents

Characters about **Animals**

cow	牛	（牛）	niú	61
horse	馬	（马）	mǎ	62
deer	鹿	（鹿）	lù	63
bear	能	（能）	néng	64
dog	犬	（犬）	quǎn	65
sheep	羊	（羊）	yáng	66
bird	鳥	（鸟）	niǎo	67
turtle	龜	（龟）	guī	68
pig	豕	（豕）	shǐ	69
rat	鼠	（鼠）	shǔ	70
snake	蛇	（蛇）	shé	71
fish	魚	（鱼）	yú	72
worm	蟲	（虫）	chóng	73
feather	羽	（羽）	yǔ	74
horn	角	（角）	jiǎo	75
claw	爪	（爪）	zhǎo	76
fly	飛	（飞）	fēi	77
wrong	非	（非）	fēi	78
nest	巢	（巢）	cháo	79

Characters about **Tools**

boat	舟	（舟）	zhōu	80
vehicle	車	（车）	chē	81
net	網	（网）	wǎng	82
umbrella	傘	（伞）	sǎn	83
bottle	酉	（酉）	yǒu	84
pen	筆	（笔）	bǐ	85
container	皿	（皿）	mǐn	86
ceramic container	缶	（缶）	fǒu	87
dipper	斗	（斗）	dǒu	88
food container	豆	（豆）	dòu	89
ruler	工	（工）	gōng	90

Characters about **Weapons**

knife	刀	（刀）	dāo	91
axe	斤	（斤）	jīn	92
arrow	矢	（矢）	shǐ	93
bow	弓	（弓）	gōng	94
dagger-axe	戈	（戈）	gē	95
reach	至	（至）	zhì	96
peace	吉	（吉）	jí	97

Characters about **Clothing**

kerchief	巾	（巾）	jīn	98
silk	絲	（丝）	sī	99
clothes	衣	（衣）	yī	100

Characters about **Housing**

cave	穴	（穴）	xué	101
window	窗	（窗）	chuāng	102
door (one frame)	戶	（户）	hù	103
door (two frame)	門	（门）	mén	104
tile	瓦	（瓦）	wǎ	105

Miscellaneous characters

west	西	（西）	xī	106
same level	齊	（齐）	qí	107
enter	入	（入）	rù	108

Combination words 109-308
(Ideatives, Harmonics, Indicatives,
Borroweds and Transmissives)

Words with **People (亻)**				
give	付	（付）	fù	109
rest	休	（休）	xiū	110
stand	立	（立）	lì	111
position	位	（位）	wèi	112
depend	依	（依）	yī	113
trust	信	（信）	xìn	114
protect	保	（保）	bǎo	115
bend over	伏	（伏）	fú	116
intimate	比	（比）	bǐ	117
north	北	（北）	běi	118
follow	從	（从）	cóng	119
crowd	眾	（众）	zhòng	120
here	此	（此）	cǐ	121
dead	死	（死）	sǐ	122
bury	葬	（葬）	zàng	123
sky	天	（天）	tiān	124
person with tattoo	文	（文）	wén	125
fight	鬥	（斗）	dòu	126
countenance	色	（色）	sè	127
arrive	到	（到）	dào	128
forward	前	（前）	qián	129
approach	即	（即）	jí	130

Words with **Heart (忄, 心)**				
character	性	（性）	xìng	131
parental love	慈	（慈）	cí	132
shame	恥	（耻）	chǐ	133
always	恆	（恒）	héng	134
a will	志	（志）	zhì	135
think	思	（思）	sī	136

Words with **Hands (扌, 又, 寸)**				
shoot	射	（射）	shè	137
friend	友	（友）	yǒu	138
lost	失	（失）	shī	139
catch up	及	（及）	jí	140
fight	爭	（争）	zhēng	141
an inch	寸	（寸）	cùn	142
accept	受	（受）	shòu	143
love	愛	（爱）	ài	144
catch	捉	（捉）	zhuō	145
pull	拉	（拉）	lā	146
put right	改	（改）	gǎi	147
offer	奉	（奉）	fèng	148
father	父	（父）	fù	149
soldier	兵	（兵）	bīng	150
drum	鼓	（鼓）	gǔ	151
skin	皮	（皮）	pí	152
leather	革	（革）	gé	153

Words with **Toes, foot (止)**				
go out	出	（出）	chū	154
return	返	（返）	fǎn	155
rightness	正	（正）	zhèng	156
exactly	是	（是）	shì	157
calm	定	（定）	dìng	158
walk	走	（走）	zǒu	159
resort to force	武	（武）	wǔ	160

Words with **Eye (目)**				
see	見	（见）	jiàn	161
see	看	（看）	kàn	162
seek	覓	（觅）	mì	163
hat	冒	（冒）	mào	164
sleep	睡	（睡）	shuì	165

ANCIENT CHARACTER	PRESENT FORM	SIMPLIFIED FORM	PRESENT MEANING
⊙	日	日	sun, day

— sun
— hottest spot

The word is a pictograph: '⊙' is the picture of the sun. Words containing '⊙' are related to sun, brightness, or seasons.

THE PROGRESSION OF THE ANCIENT CHARACTER TO PRESENT CHARACTER | PRONUNCIATION

| ⊙ ⊖ 日 日 ⊖ 日 | rì |

中國文字

2

ANCIENT CHARACTER	PRESENT FORM	SIMPLIFIED FORM	PRESENT MEANING
⟨D⟩	月	月	moon

 sparkly highlight or reflection

The ambiguous outline indicates the round but incomplete shape of the moon. The word is a pictograph.

THE PROGRESSION OF THE ANCIENT CHARACTER TO PRESENT CHARACTER | PRONUNCIATION

♪ ♪ ⟨D⟩ ⟨⊙⟩ 夕 月 月 月	yuè

3

ANCIENT CHARACTER	PRESENT FORM	SIMPLIFIED FORM	PRESENT MEANING
⛰	山	山	hill, mountain

The word is a picture of three mountains rising from the ground.
It is a pictograph.

THE PROGRESSION OF THE ANCIENT CHARACTER TO PRESENT CHARACTER | **PRONUNCIATION**

| ⛰ 𝓦 𝕎 𝕎 𝔀 ⩗ 𝙒 山 | shān |

中國文字

4

ANCIENT CHARACTER	PRESENT FORM	SIMPLIFIED FORM	PRESENT MEANING
川	水	水	water

'川' is like the flow of water. The word is a pictograph.

THE PROGRESSION OF THE ANCIENT CHARACTER TO PRESENT CHARACTER

PRONUNCIATION

川 川 川 氵 水	shuǐ

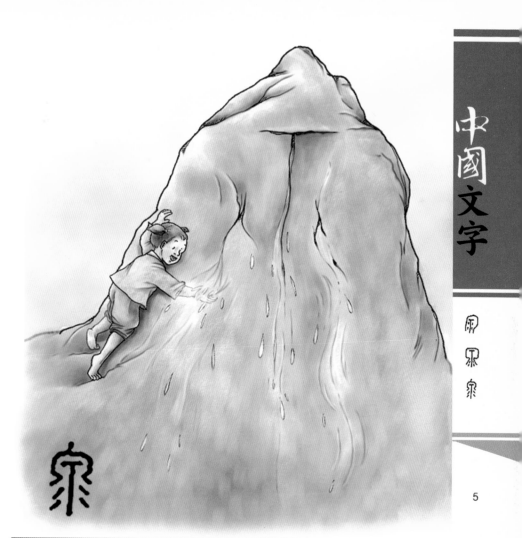

ANCIENT CHARACTER	PRESENT FORM	SIMPLIFIED FORM	PRESENT MEANING
泉	泉	泉	spring, source

泉 — rock
— cracks
— water

It is a pictograph of water flowing from the cracks of a rock or mountain.

THE PROGRESSION OF THE ANCIENT CHARACTER TO PRESENT CHARACTER | **PRONUNCIATION**

| 泉 屌 泉 泉 泉 | quán |

中國文字

6

ANCIENT CHARACTER	PRESENT FORM	SIMPLIFIED FORM	PRESENT MEANING
火	火	火	fire

The word is like hot white flame rising from the objects it destroys. It is a pictograph.

THE PROGRESSION OF THE ANCIENT CHARACTER TO PRESENT CHARACTER	PRONUNCIATION
火 火 火 火 火	huǒ

ANCIENT CHARACTER	PRESENT FORM	SIMPLIFIED FORM	PRESENT MEANING
土	土	土	soil

Soil was considered the essence of life that gave birth to numerous things. '土' looks like the root of a plant that goes into a deep layer of soil and prospers. The word is a pictograph.

THE PROGRESSION OF THE ANCIENT CHARACTER TO PRESENT CHARACTER | **PRONUNCIATION**

| ♫ 𝌀 ⛐ 𐊫 土 土 土 | tǔ |

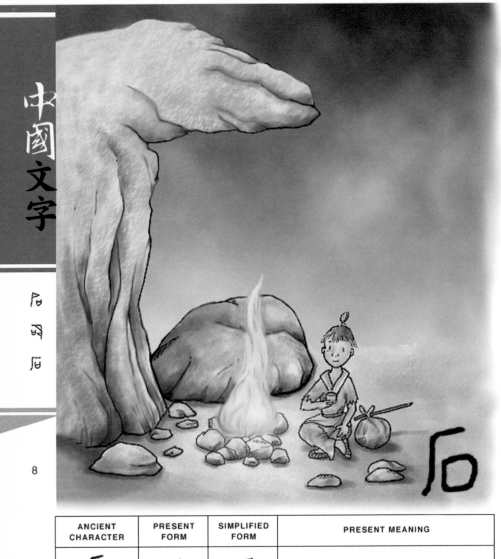

8

ANCIENT CHARACTER	PRESENT FORM	SIMPLIFIED FORM	PRESENT MEANING
石	石	石	stone, rock

It is a pictograph: ' 厂 ' is a cliff, ' 口 ' is a rock.
Rocks can be found under a cliff.

THE PROGRESSION OF THE ANCIENT CHARACTER TO PRESENT CHARACTER	PRONUNCIATION
石 石 石 石 石 石	shí

雨
雨
雨

9

雨

ANCIENT CHARACTER	PRESENT FORM	SIMPLIFIED FORM	PRESENT MEANING
雨	雨	雨	rain

It is a pictograph: ' ⌐ ' is like the sky, ' ∏ ' is like a cloud, ' 仌 ' is like raindrops. Rain is from the cloud in the sky.

THE PROGRESSION OF THE ANCIENT CHARACTER TO PRESENT CHARACTER **PRONUNCIATION**

雨 雨 雨 雨 雨 雨 雨 雨	yǔ

ፔ
◎
ፔ

10

ANCIENT CHARACTER	PRESENT FORM	SIMPLIFIED FORM	PRESENT MEANING
 ⊙	回	回	return, turn round

It is a pictograph: '⊙' is like a swirl with waves rotating towards its center. The original meaning was 'whirl'.

THE PROGRESSION OF THE ANCIENT CHARACTER TO PRESENT CHARACTER | PRONUNCIATION

| ᄃ ᄃ ⊙ ◎ ⓐ 回 | huí |

ANCIENT CHARACTER	PRESENT FORM	SIMPLIFIED FORM	PRESENT MEANING
仌	冰	冰	ice, feel cold

It is a pictograph: '仌' is the pattern on ice.
Later, water is added to the side '仌⺡' to indicate that '仌⺡ ice' is the
solid form of water.

THE PROGRESSION OF THE ANCIENT CHARACTER TO PRESENT CHARACTER	PRONUNCIATION
仌 仌⺡ ⺀ 冰	bīng

ANCIENT CHARACTER	PRESENT FORM	SIMPLIFIED FORM	PRESENT MEANING
雲	雲	云	cloud

rain—雲
—swirl of the wet air

'雲' was believed to be the moist turbulence around hills or mountains that would bring in rain.
'⌒' is a pictograph.

THE PROGRESSION OF THE ANCIENT CHARACTER TO PRESENT CHARACTER | **PRONUNCIATION**

雲 雲 | yún

丰
王
玉

ANCIENT CHARACTER	PRESENT FORM	SIMPLIFIED FORM	PRESENT MEANING
王	玉	玉	jade

王 — jade — 王

It is a pictograph: '王' looks like three pieces of jade linked together.

THE PROGRESSION OF THE ANCIENT CHARACTER TO PRESENT CHARACTER	PRONUNCIATION
丰 王 王 玉	yù

中國文字

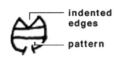

ANCIENT CHARACTER	PRESENT FORM	SIMPLIFIED FORM	PRESENT MEANING
𤕫	貝	贝	shellfish, cowry

indented edges — pattern

'𤕫' is a special kind of shell with indented edges and beautiful patterns. They were valuable jewels and currency of the time. Words containing '𤕫' link with money.
'𤕫' is a pictograph.

THE PROGRESSION OF THE ANCIENT CHARACTER TO PRESENT CHARACTER

PRONUNCIATION
bèi

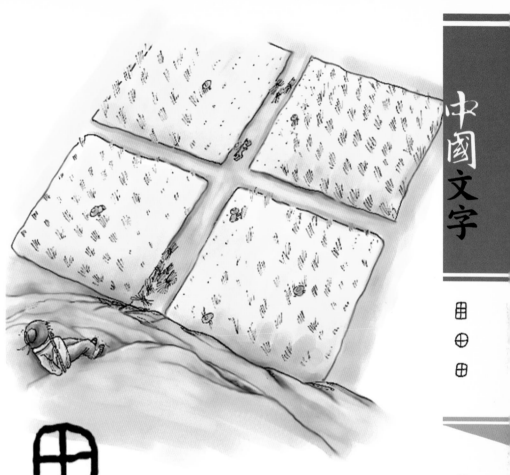

ANCIENT CHARACTER	PRESENT FORM	SIMPLIFIED FORM	PRESENT MEANING
田	田	田	field, farmland, cropland

It is a pictograph: '田' is a field where crops are planted. '十' are paths on the field.

THE PROGRESSION OF THE ANCIENT CHARACTER TO PRESENT CHARACTER | PRONUNCIATION
| 田 田 田 田 田 田 | tián |

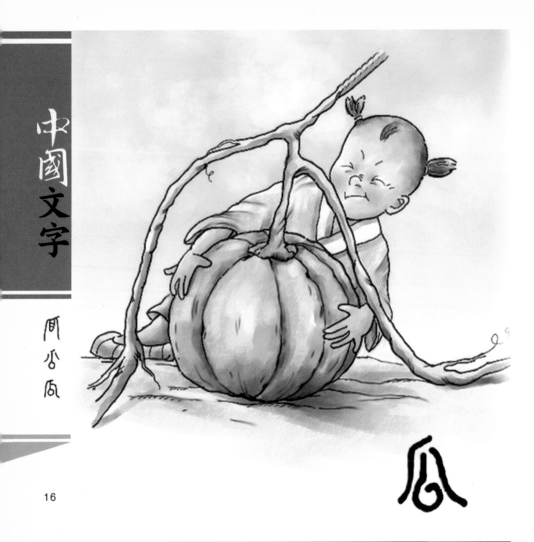

中國文字

16

ANCIENT CHARACTER	PRESENT FORM	SIMPLIFIED FORM	PRESENT MEANING
瓜	瓜	瓜	squash, melon, gourd

' 𠯑 ' is the squash which is attached to the stalk.

THE PROGRESSION OF THE ANCIENT CHARACTER TO PRESENT CHARACTER	PRONUNCIATION
瓜 瓜 瓜 瓜 瓜	guā

ANCIENT CHARACTER	PRESENT FORM	SIMPLIFIED FORM	PRESENT MEANING
禾	禾	禾	standing grain (esp. rice)

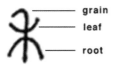

— grain
— leaf
— root

It is a pictograph: '禾' looks like a rice plant with rice grains, leaves and root.

THE PROGRESSION OF THE ANCIENT CHARACTER TO PRESENT CHARACTER	PRONUNCIATION
禾 禾 禾 禾 禾 禾	hé

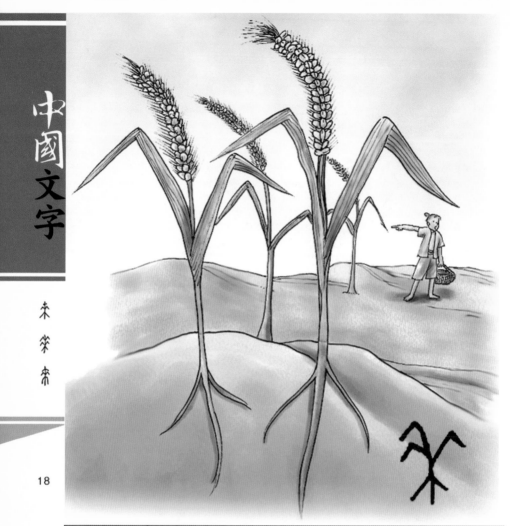

18

ANCIENT CHARACTER	PRESENT FORM	SIMPLIFIED FORM	PRESENT MEANING
來	來	来	come, arrive

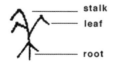

— stalk
— leaf
— root

The word is a pictograph. '來' is the old word for wheat. Later, it was used most often to mean 'come', so another word was made for 'wheat'.

wheat becomes '麥'. (p.228)

THE PROGRESSION OF THE ANCIENT CHARACTER TO PRESENT CHARACTER | PRONUNCIATION

| 來 來 來 來 來 來 | lái |

ANCIENT CHARACTER	PRESENT FORM	SIMPLIFIED FORM	PRESENT MEANING
米	米	米	rice

— grain

It is a pictograph: '米' looks like the grains of rice crops.

THE PROGRESSION OF THE ANCIENT CHARACTER TO PRESENT CHARACTER

	PRONUNCIATION
米 米 米 米 米 米	mǐ

中國文字

ANCIENT CHARACTER	PRESENT FORM	SIMPLIFIED FORM	PRESENT MEANING
垂	垂	垂	hang down, let fall

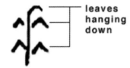 leaves hanging down

It is a pictograph: a plant with its leaves hanging down in a state of suspension. Later, '土 soil' was added to its base indicating clearly that it is a plant.

THE PROGRESSION OF THE ANCIENT CHARACTER TO PRESENT CHARACTER   **PRONUNCIATION**

垂 垂 垂 垚 垂	chuí

中國文字

竹
𥫗
竹

21

ANCIENT CHARACTER	PRESENT FORM	SIMPLIFIED FORM	PRESENT MEANING
个个	竹	竹	bamboo

— leaf

— stalk

It is a pictograph: '个个' looks like a plant with straight stalks and spiked leaves.
Words containing '个个' relate to bamboo products.

THE PROGRESSION OF THE ANCIENT CHARACTER TO PRESENT CHARACTER

	PRONUNCIATION
竹 个个 𥬠 竹 艸 竹	zhú

中國文字

22

ANCIENT CHARACTER	PRESENT FORM	SIMPLIFIED FORM	PRESENT MEANING
米	木	木	tree, timber, wood, made of wood, wooden

— branches

— roots

It is a pictograph: '米' looks like a tree springing from the soil with branches stretching upward and outward. The lower part looks like roots deeply buried in soil for support.

THE PROGRESSION OF THE ANCIENT CHARACTER TO PRESENT CHARACTER	PRONUNCIATION
朿 米 米 朿 木	mù

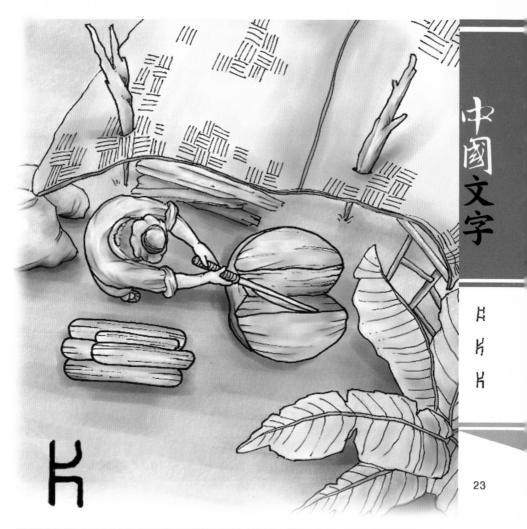

ANCIENT CHARACTER	PRESENT FORM	SIMPLIFIED FORM	PRESENT MEANING
爿 爿	片	片	thin piece, slice, flake

— a slice

— stump

'片' is rotated 90 degrees

It is a pictograph: '爿' or '片' is half of '木 wood'. It means a stump is cut in slices.

THE PROGRESSION OF THE ANCIENT CHARACTER TO PRESENT CHARACTER — PRONUNCIATION

THE PROGRESSION OF THE ANCIENT CHARACTER TO PRESENT CHARACTER	PRONUNCIATION
片 片 片 片	piàn

果
果
果

ANCIENT CHARACTER	PRESENT FORM	SIMPLIFIED FORM	PRESENT MEANING
果	果	果	fruit

果 — seed
　 — fruit
　 — tree

It is a pictograph: '果 fruits' are on a tree.

THE PROGRESSION OF THE ANCIENT CHARACTER TO PRESENT CHARACTER	PRONUNCIATION
果　果　果　果	guǒ

25

ANCIENT CHARACTER	PRESENT FORM	SIMPLIFIED FORM	PRESENT MEANING
白	白	白	white

White is the color of rice. The word 'white' refers to the shape of a grain of rice. '白' is a pictograph of rice.

THE PROGRESSION OF THE ANCIENT CHARACTER TO PRESENT CHARACTER	PRONUNCIATION
白 白 白 白 白	bái

26

ANCIENT CHARACTER	PRESENT FORM	SIMPLIFIED FORM	PRESENT MEANING
屮	生	生	give birth to, grow, alive

It is a pictograph: '屮' looks like a plant growing up from the soil.

THE PROGRESSION OF THE ANCIENT CHARACTER TO PRESENT CHARACTER	PRONUNCIATION
屮 屮 屮 生 生 生	shēng

ANCIENT CHARACTER	PRESENT FORM	SIMPLIFIED FORM	PRESENT MEANING
凸	凸	凸	protruding, raised

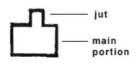

— jut

— main portion

It is a pictograph: '凸' is like a jut that extends beyond the main portion.

THE PROGRESSION OF THE ANCIENT CHARACTER TO PRESENT CHARACTER	PRONUNCIATION
凸	tū

28

ANCIENT CHARACTER	PRESENT FORM	SIMPLIFIED FORM	PRESENT MEANING
凹	凹	凹	concave, hollow, sunken, dented

hollow
main portion

It is a pictograph: '凹' is like a hollow that is indented in the main portion.

THE PROGRESSION OF THE ANCIENT CHARACTER TO PRESENT CHARACTER	PRONUNCIATION
凹	āo

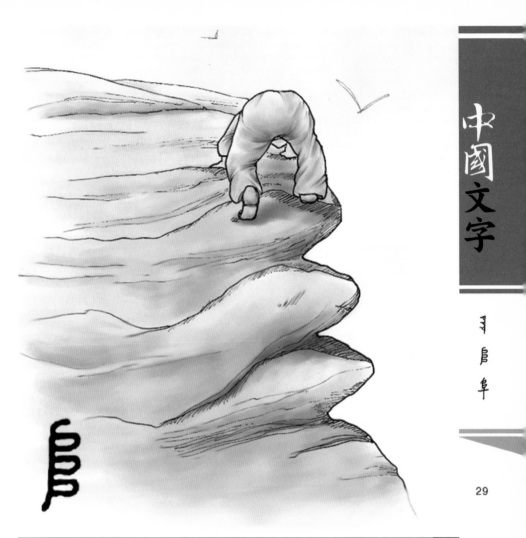

ANCIENT CHARACTER	PRESENT FORM	SIMPLIFIED FORM	PRESENT MEANING
𨸏	阜 阝	阜	mound

It is a pictograph: '阜' looks like the indented area of a cliff or mountain. Words containing '阝' (on the left side of a word) mean something related to the height of land. e.g. '降 descend', '墬 fall'.

THE PROGRESSION OF THE ANCIENT CHARACTER TO PRESENT CHARACTER	PRONUNCIATION
𠂤 𨸏 阜	fù

30

ANCIENT CHARACTER	PRESENT FORM	SIMPLIFIED FORM	PRESENT MEANING
彳	行	行	go, go on foot

彳 — the intersection of a road

It is a pictograph: '彳' is like a map showing a cross road that leads in different directions.

THE PROGRESSION OF THE ANCIENT CHARACTER TO PRESENT CHARACTER | PRONUNCIATION

| 彳 彳 彳 彳 彳 行 | xíng |

ANCIENT CHARACTER	PRESENT FORM	SIMPLIFIED FORM	PRESENT MEANING
尺	人	人	person, people, human beings

It is a pictograph. '人' is like a man walking. Human beings were considered to be the most precious species on earth, each possessing both soul and characters.

THE PROGRESSION OF THE ANCIENT CHARACTER TO PRESENT CHARACTER	PRONUNCIATION
亻 人 尺 人	rén

中國文字

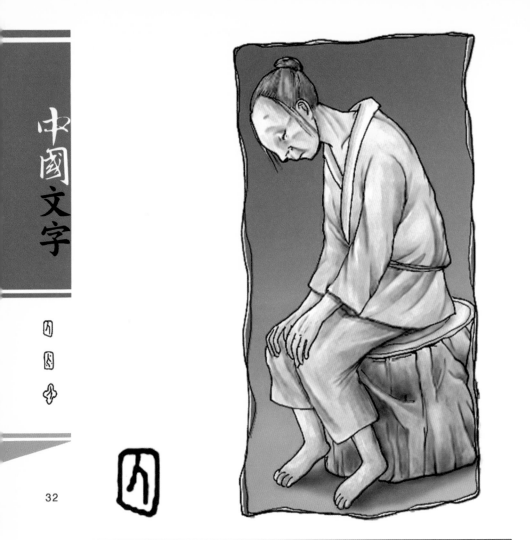

32

ANCIENT CHARACTER	PRESENT FORM	SIMPLIFIED FORM	PRESENT MEANING
囚	囚	囚	imprison, prisoner

It is a pictograph. '囚' combines '囗 a confined area', and '人 a person'. A person was confined.

THE PROGRESSION OF THE ANCIENT CHARACTER TO PRESENT CHARACTER

	PRONUNCIATION
囚 囚 囚 囚 囚 囚	qiú

33

ANCIENT CHARACTER	PRESENT FORM	SIMPLIFIED FORM	PRESENT MEANING
	包	包	wrap, bundle, package

— embryonic membrane

— fetus

The word is a pictograph: '' is like a fetus which is surrounded by an embryonic membrane, safely in its mother's womb. The original meaning of '' is embryonic membrane.

THE PROGRESSION OF THE ANCIENT CHARACTER TO PRESENT CHARACTER | PRONUNCIATION

|  包 包 包 包 | bāo |

ANCIENT CHARACTER	PRESENT FORM	SIMPLIFIED FORM	PRESENT MEANING
𡠟	女	女	woman, female, daughter

It is a pictograph. Most women stayed at home in olden times. The word is like the posture of a woman kneeling quietly with both hands crossed and resting on her thighs.

THE PROGRESSION OF THE ANCIENT CHARACTER TO PRESENT CHARACTER　　**PRONUNCIATION**

𡠟　帇　㚢　女	nǚ

ANCIENT CHARACTER	PRESENT FORM	SIMPLIFIED FORM	PRESENT MEANING
兒	兒	儿	little child, son

'兒' looks like a baby with its skull not yet fused together. It is a pictograph.

the opening of the skull of a baby

THE PROGRESSION OF THE ANCIENT CHARACTER TO PRESENT CHARACTER	PRONUNCIATION
兒 兒 兒 兒 兒	ér

ANCIENT CHARACTER	PRESENT FORM	SIMPLIFIED FORM	PRESENT MEANING
孑	子	子	child, son

It is a pictograph. It is like a child who barely knows how to walk but happily throwing his arms up and down.

THE PROGRESSION OF THE ANCIENT CHARACTER TO PRESENT CHARACTER	PRONUNCIATION
孑 界 孑 专 孑 孚 孕 子 子	zǐ

ANCIENT CHARACTER	PRESENT FORM	SIMPLIFIED FORM	PRESENT MEANING
大	大	大	big, large, great, main, heavy (rain), strong (wind)

The word is a pictograph. '大' looks like a man stretching out his arms and legs. The ancient Chinese thought that the sky was big(great), the earth was big(great) and humans could be big(great) too. Therefore '大 big' takes the form of a man.

THE PROGRESSION OF THE ANCIENT CHARACTER TO PRESENT CHARACTER	PRONUNCIATION
大 大 大 大 大 大	dà

38

ANCIENT CHARACTER	PRESENT FORM	SIMPLIFIED FORM	PRESENT MEANING
身	身	身	body

It is a pictograph. The word is like the side view of a pregnant woman's body.

THE PROGRESSION OF THE ANCIENT CHARACTER TO PRESENT CHARACTER | PRONUNCIATION

身 身 身 身 身 身 身 身	shēn

ANCIENT CHARACTER	PRESENT FORM	SIMPLIFIED FORM	PRESENT MEANING
〣	氣	气	gas, breath, spirit, vigor, atmosphere

'〣' is a pictograph: it looks like hot steam coming from a bowl of soup. It originally meant air, gas, steam, and also the air emitted from the body. '〣' is the basic element that fills the earth; it then implies the atmosphere of a place. Besides, it is an important substance that goes in and out of a human body, it also reflects the physical and psychological state of a person.

THE PROGRESSION OF THE ANCIENT CHARACTER TO PRESENT CHARACTER | PRONUNCIATION

| 〣 三 ⺈ ⺈ ⻖ 气 | qì |

內

ANCIENT CHARACTER	PRESENT FORM	SIMPLIFIED FORM	PRESENT MEANING
內	內	內	inner, inside, within

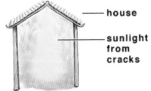
— house

— sunlight from cracks

It is a pictograph: '內' means there is something entering from outside. One study said that it is a picture of sunlight entering through a crack in the roof.

THE PROGRESSION OF THE ANCIENT CHARACTER TO PRESENT CHARACTER   **PRONUNCIATION**

內 內 內 內 內 內 內	nèi

41

ANCIENT CHARACTER	PRESENT FORM	SIMPLIFIED FORM	PRESENT MEANING
長	長	长	long, length, (time) of long duration, be strong in

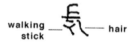

walking stick — hair

It is a pictograph. '長' is like an old man with long hair holding a walking stick.

THE PROGRESSION OF THE ANCIENT CHARACTER TO PRESENT CHARACTER | PRONUNCIATION

| 耂 耂 耂 長 長 耂 長 長 | cháng |

42

ANCIENT CHARACTER	PRESENT FORM	SIMPLIFIED FORM	PRESENT MEANING
∃	又	又	again, and

∃ —— finger
—— hand

It is a pictograph: '∃' looks like a right hand with three fingers. Words containing '∃' are related to the use of hands to accomplish something, like '取 take', and '受 accept'.

THE PROGRESSION OF THE ANCIENT CHARACTER TO PRESENT CHARACTER | PRONUNCIATION

| ∃ | ∃ | ∀ | 又 | ∃ | 又 | yòu |

中國文字

ANCIENT CHARACTER	PRESENT FORM	SIMPLIFIED FORM	PRESENT MEANING
㐱 㝈	欠	欠	owe, be behind with, insufficient, yawn

㝈 —— mouth
　 —— sitter

㐱 —— breath
　 —— sitter

'㝈' looks like a person sitting on his knees, opening his mouth widely and exhaling.
'㐱' looks like a sitter with breath coming out from his mouth -- he is yawning.
The word is a pictograph.

THE PROGRESSION OF THE ANCIENT CHARACTER TO PRESENT CHARACTER　　PRONUNCIATION

㝈 㝈 㐱 欠	qiàn

中國文字

ㅂ ◌ ◌

44

ANCIENT CHARACTER	PRESENT FORM	SIMPLIFIED FORM	PRESENT MEANING
ㅂ	ㅁ	ㅁ	mouth, rim, opening

' ㅂ ' is a pictograph: It is like the shape of an open mouth.

THE PROGRESSION OF THE ANCIENT CHARACTER TO PRESENT CHARACTER | PRONUNCIATION

ㅂ ㅂ ◌ ㅂ ㅁ | kǒu

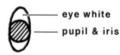

中國文字

45

ANCIENT CHARACTER	PRESENT FORM	SIMPLIFIED FORM	PRESENT MEANING
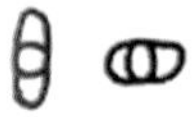 𐅃 ⬭	目	目	eye

— eye white
— pupil & iris

' 𐅃 ' is a pictograph.
It is a picture of an eye.

THE PROGRESSION OF THE ANCIENT CHARACTER TO PRESENT CHARACTER | PRONUNCIATION

𐅃 𐅃 𐅃 𐅃 𐅃 𐅃 ⬭ 目 目	mù

ANCIENT CHARACTER	PRESENT FORM	SIMPLIFIED FORM	PRESENT MEANING
弓	耳	耳	ear

to auditory canal ——— 弓

' 弓 ' is a pictograph.
The word is like an ear.

THE PROGRESSION OF THE ANCIENT CHARACTER TO PRESENT CHARACTER | PRONUNCIATION

| 弓 弓 弓 弓 耳 耳 耳 耳 | ěr |

ANCIENT CHARACTER	PRESENT FORM	SIMPLIFIED FORM	PRESENT MEANING
自	自	自	self, oneself, one's own, from, since

The original meaning of '自' was nose, and it is a pictograph of a nose. A person would point to his nose when he wanted to indicate that the object belonged to him or that it was he who had done something. So '自' comes to mean 'me'.

THE PROGRESSION OF THE ANCIENT CHARACTER TO PRESENT CHARACTER	PRONUNCIATION
自 自 自 自 自 自 自	zì

中國文字

48

ANCIENT CHARACTER	PRESENT FORM	SIMPLIFIED FORM	PRESENT MEANING
手	手	手	hand

palm — fingers

The word is a picture of a hand, it is a pictograph.

THE PROGRESSION OF THE ANCIENT CHARACTER TO PRESENT CHARACTER | PRONUNCIATION

shǒu

49

ANCIENT CHARACTER	PRESENT FORM	SIMPLIFIED FORM	PRESENT MEANING
止	止	止	stop, cease, discontinue

'止' is like a foot print in the sand with toes clearly seen.
It is a pictograph. Words containing '止' relate to walking.
For example: '步 a step' and '涉 wade'.
However, we cease walking by stopping the movement of our feet,
therefore, the word came to mean 'stop' at later stage.

THE PROGRESSION OF THE ANCIENT CHARACTER TO PRESENT CHARACTER | PRONUNCIATION

| 止 止 止 止 止 止 止 | zhǐ |

ANCIENT CHARACTER	PRESENT FORM	SIMPLIFIED FORM	PRESENT MEANING
足	足	足	foot, leg

'止' is toes, 'ㅁ' is knee cap.
Toes connected to knee cap implies leg.
The word is a pictograph.

THE PROGRESSION OF THE ANCIENT CHARACTER TO PRESENT CHARACTER	PRONUNCIATION
足 足 足 足 足 足 足	zú

己
己
己

己

51

ANCIENT CHARACTER	PRESENT FORM	SIMPLIFIED FORM	PRESENT MEANING
己	己	己	oneself, one's own

'己' is a place where someone can hide or rest, and it is also like the intestines of a human being. It, therefore, implies oneself. The word is a pictograph.

THE PROGRESSION OF THE ANCIENT CHARACTER TO PRESENT CHARACTER	PRONUNCIATION
己 己 己 己 己 己	jǐ

中國文字

52

ANCIENT CHARACTER	PRESENT FORM	SIMPLIFIED FORM	PRESENT MEANING
屮	心	心	The heart, mind, intention

artery ———
ventricle ———

The word is a pictograph which is like the shape of a heart with arteries and ventricles.

THE PROGRESSION OF THE ANCIENT CHARACTER TO PRESENT CHARACTER	PRONUNCIATION
屮 屮 屮 屮 屮 屮 心	xīn

53

ANCIENT CHARACTER	PRESENT FORM	SIMPLIFIED FORM	PRESENT MEANING
	首	首	head, first, leader

—— hair

nose is the important feature in the face

It is a pictograph of a person's head (a nose was used to stand for other features on the face). Its original meaning was 'head'.
Since head is on the top of a person's body, and the head is seen first when a baby is born, it then also be used as 'first'.

THE PROGRESSION OF THE ANCIENT CHARACTER TO PRESENT CHARACTER   **PRONUNCIATION**

	shǒu

54

ANCIENT CHARACTER	PRESENT FORM	SIMPLIFIED FORM	PRESENT MEANING
𦣻	頁	页	page

'𦣻' combines '𦣻 head' and '屮 sitting posture'. It is a pictograph of a sitter with his head clearly seen. Words containing '頁' relate to 'head'. Its original meaning was 'head'. Later, it was used for the meaning of 'page' (page is like a face that needs to be studied. 'Page 頁' is a transmissive.)
Another word for head '頭' was made.

THE PROGRESSION OF THE ANCIENT CHARACTER TO PRESENT CHARACTER	PRONUNCIATION
𦣻 𦣻 𦣻 頁 頁	yè

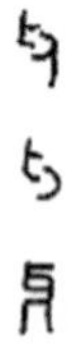

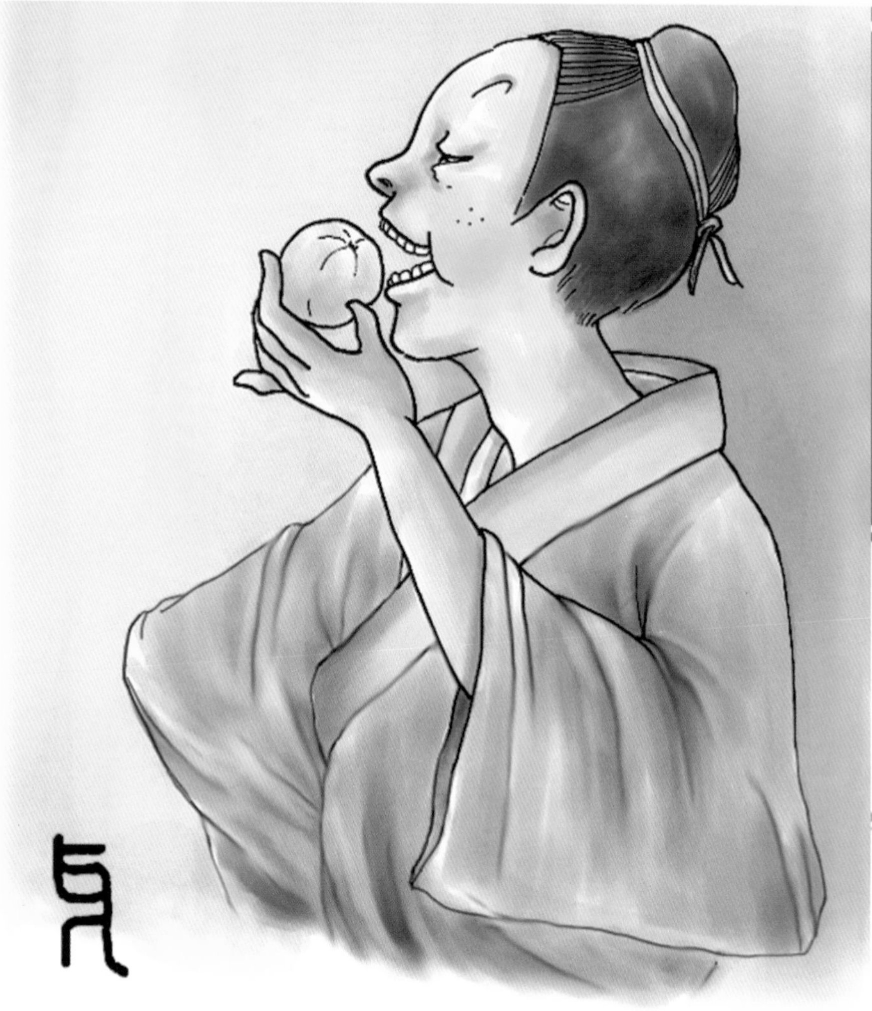

ANCIENT CHARACTER	PRESENT FORM	SIMPLIFIED FORM	PRESENT MEANING
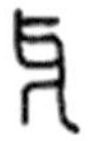	牙	牙	tooth

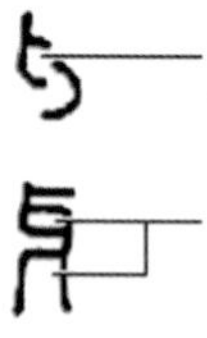

teeth with grinding motion
teeth

'' looks like teeth from the upper and lower jaws. It is a pictograph.

THE PROGRESSION OF THE ANCIENT CHARACTER TO PRESENT CHARACTER	PRONUNCIATION
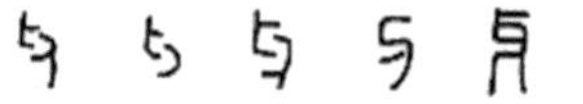 牙	yá

中國文字

56

ANCIENT CHARACTER	PRESENT FORM	SIMPLIFIED FORM	PRESENT MEANING
𦥑 𣥂	齒	齿	tooth

— front teeth

'𦥑' is a pictograph: It looks like an open mouth with four front teeth. Its original meaning was front teeth. Later the word '止' was put on top of '𦥑' because '𦥑' sounds like '止'.

THE PROGRESSION OF THE ANCIENT CHARACTER TO PRESENT CHARACTER | PRONUNCIATION

| | | | | | | | | chǐ |

ANCIENT CHARACTER	PRESENT FORM	SIMPLIFIED FORM	PRESENT MEANING
	舌	舌	tongue

— tongue
— movement of tongue
— saliva spill out
— mouth

The word is a pictograph: ' ' is like a tongue sticking out from one's mouth and saliva spilling around when that person is speaking.

THE PROGRESSION OF THE ANCIENT CHARACTER TO PRESENT CHARACTER	PRONUNCIATION
	shé

ANCIENT CHARACTER	PRESENT FORM	SIMPLIFIED FORM	PRESENT MEANING
肉	肉	肉	meat, flesh

' 肉 ' looks like a piece of meat with texture in it. It is a pictograph. Words containing ' 肉 ' relate to the bodies of humans or animals.

THE PROGRESSION OF THE ANCIENT CHARACTER TO PRESENT CHARACTER	PRONUNCIATION
夕 夕 月 月 月 肉	ròu

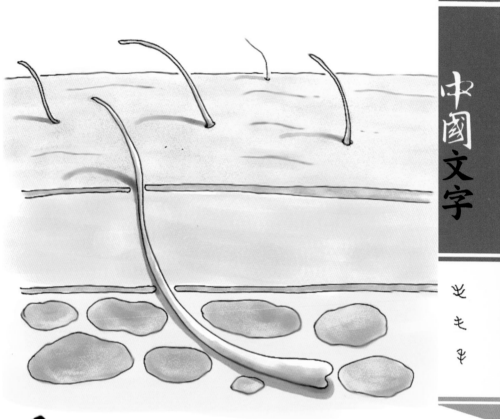

ANCIENT CHARACTER	PRESENT FORM	SIMPLIFIED FORM	PRESENT MEANING
毛	毛	毛	hair, feather

 surface of skin
inner skin
hair

'毛' looks like one end of hair extends from the surface of the skin while the other end is buried deeply down below two skin layers. It is a pictograph.

THE PROGRESSION OF THE ANCIENT CHARACTER TO PRESENT CHARACTER	PRONUNCIATION
毛 毛 毛 毛 毛 毛	máo

60

ANCIENT CHARACTER	PRESENT FORM	SIMPLIFIED FORM	PRESENT MEANING
冎	骨	骨	bone

bones work as a frame for the body

'冎' is a pictograph which illustrates the frame for supporting a body.
Later, '肉 flesh' was added to the word, emphasis was given to the relationship between flesh and bone.

THE PROGRESSION OF THE ANCIENT CHARACTER TO PRESENT CHARACTER | **PRONUNCIATION**

gǔ

ㄓ
ㄓ
ㄓ

61

ANCIENT CHARACTER	PRESENT FORM	SIMPLIFIED FORM	PRESENT MEANING
ㄓ	牛	牛	ox, cow, cattle

The word looks like the head of a cow with two curved horns.
It is a pictograph.

THE PROGRESSION OF THE ANCIENT CHARACTER TO PRESENT CHARACTER	PRONUNCIATION
ㄓ ㄓ ㄓ 牜 牛 牛	niú

中國文字

62

ANCIENT CHARACTER	PRESENT FORM	SIMPLIFIED FORM	PRESENT MEANING
馬	馬	马	horse

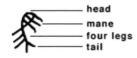

head
mane
four legs
tail

'馬' looks like a horse with a head, mane, four legs and a tail.
The word is a pictograph.

THE PROGRESSION OF THE ANCIENT CHARACTER TO PRESENT CHARACTER **PRONUNCIATION**

馬 馬 馬 馬 馬 馬 馬 馬	mǎ

ANCIENT CHARACTER	PRESENT FORM	SIMPLIFIED FORM	PRESENT MEANING
麤	鹿	鹿	deer

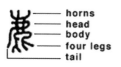
— horns
— head
— body
— four legs
— tail

'麤' looks exactly like a deer with two horns, a head, a body, four legs and a tail. The word is a pictograph.

THE PROGRESSION OF THE ANCIENT CHARACTER TO PRESENT CHARACTER | PRONUNCIATION

lù

ANCIENT CHARACTER	PRESENT FORM	SIMPLIFIED FORM	PRESENT MEANING
能	能	能	ability, capability, skill

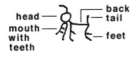

head — mouth with teeth — back — tail — feet

The original meaning of '能' was 'bear'. Bear is big, strong and powerful. By extension, it means someone who is capable. The word is a pictograph.

Bear is now written as '熊'.

THE PROGRESSION OF THE ANCIENT CHARACTER TO PRESENT CHARACTER   PRONUNCIATION

| 能 能 暴 能 能 能 | néng |

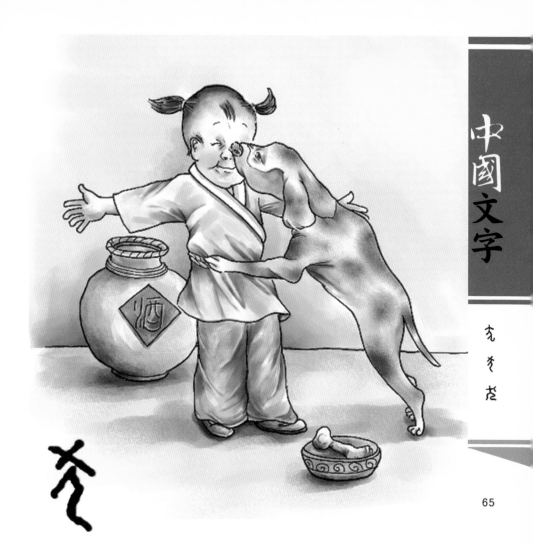

ANCIENT CHARACTER	PRESENT FORM	SIMPLIFIED FORM	PRESENT MEANING
犬	犬	犬	dog

'犬' looks like a dog bouncing or jumping up to catch something. It is a pictograph of a dog.

THE PROGRESSION OF THE ANCIENT CHARACTER TO PRESENT CHARACTER	PRONUNCIATION
犬 犬 犬 犬	quǎn

66

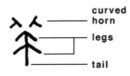

ANCIENT CHARACTER	PRESENT FORM	SIMPLIFIED FORM	PRESENT MEANING
羊	羊	羊	sheep

curved horn — legs — tail

'羊' resembles an animal with four legs, a tail, and two curved horns which are typical of sheep. The word is a pictograph of a sheep.

THE PROGRESSION OF THE ANCIENT CHARACTER TO PRESENT CHARACTER

PRONUNCIATION

yáng

ANCIENT CHARACTER	PRESENT FORM	SIMPLIFIED FORM	PRESENT MEANING
	鳥	鸟	bird

— head of bird
— feather in the neck
— feather in the wings
— tail
— legs

'' is a pictograph of a bird.

THE PROGRESSION OF THE ANCIENT CHARACTER TO PRESENT CHARACTER

PRONUNCIATION

niǎo

中國文字

68

ANCIENT CHARACTER	PRESENT FORM	SIMPLIFIED FORM	PRESENT MEANING
	龜	龟	tortoise, turtle

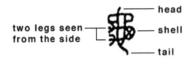

two legs seen from the side — head — shell — tail

'   ' looks exactly like the side view of a turtle with a head, a shell covering its body, two legs, and a tail. The word is a pictograph.

THE PROGRESSION OF THE ANCIENT CHARACTER TO PRESENT CHARACTER   PRONUNCIATION

	gui

豕

69

ANCIENT CHARACTER	PRESENT FORM	SIMPLIFIED FORM	PRESENT MEANING
豕	豕	豕	pig

long snout —
tail —
legs —

豕

'豕' looks like a fat animal with a long snout, four legs, and a tail. It is a pictograph of a pig.

THE PROGRESSION OF THE ANCIENT CHARACTER TO PRESENT CHARACTER	PRONUNCIATION
豕 豕 豕 豕 豕	shǐ

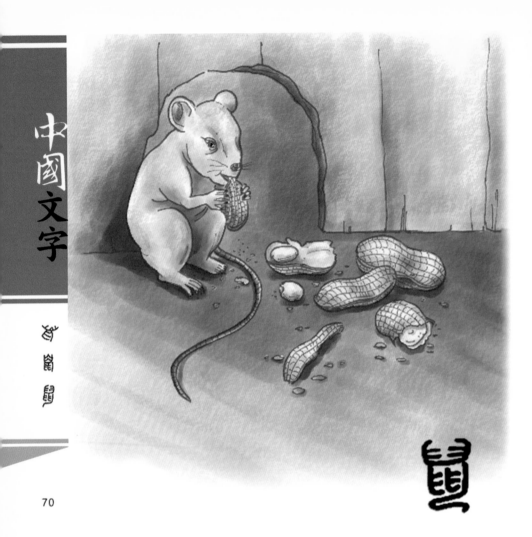

中國文字

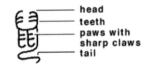

70

ANCIENT CHARACTER	PRESENT FORM	SIMPLIFIED FORM	PRESENT MEANING
鼠	鼠	鼠	mouse, rat

head
teeth
paws with
sharp claws
tail

'鼠' is a pictograph of a mouse.

THE PROGRESSION OF THE ANCIENT CHARACTER TO PRESENT CHARACTER   PRONUNCIATION

鼠	鼠	鼠	鼠	shǔ

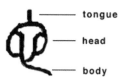

ANCIENT CHARACTER	PRESENT FORM	SIMPLIFIED FORM	PRESENT MEANING
虫	蛇	蛇	snake

— tongue

— head

— body

Snake has a triangular head and a curly body. The word is a pictograph. Later ' 虫 worm' was added to its side because snakes were thought to belong to the worm family.

THE PROGRESSION OF THE ANCIENT CHARACTER TO PRESENT CHARACTER	PRONUNCIATION
𠂤 𠂤 虫 虫 虫 虫 蚺 蛇	shé

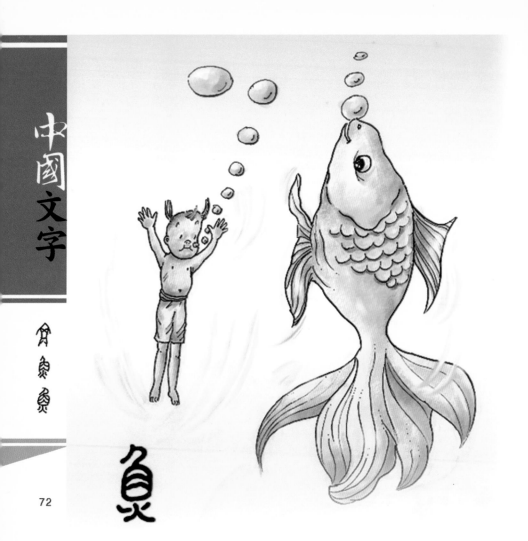

ANCIENT CHARACTER	PRESENT FORM	SIMPLIFIED FORM	PRESENT MEANING
魚	魚	鱼	fish

— head
— body
— scales
— tail

The word is a picture of a fish.
'魚' is a pictograph.

THE PROGRESSION OF THE ANCIENT CHARACTER TO PRESENT CHARACTER	PRONUNCIATION
魚 魚 魚 魚 魚	yú

ANCIENT CHARACTER	PRESENT FORM	SIMPLIFIED FORM	PRESENT MEANING
 它	蟲	虫	worm

head
body

It looks like an elongated, soft-bodied worm coming out of the soil. '它' is a pictograph.

THE PROGRESSION OF THE ANCIENT CHARACTER TO PRESENT CHARACTER

PRONUNCIATION

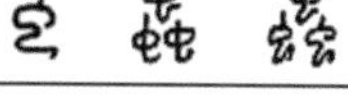

chóng

中國文字

74

ANCIENT CHARACTER	PRESENT FORM	SIMPLIFIED FORM	PRESENT MEANING
翂	羽	羽	feather

翂 — feather

The word looks like two feathers arranged together. It is a pictograph of two feathers.

THE PROGRESSION OF THE ANCIENT CHARACTER TO PRESENT CHARACTER | **PRONUNCIATION**

| 羽 羽 仴 羽 羽 翂 羽 羽 | yǔ |

中國文字

75

ANCIENT CHARACTER	PRESENT FORM	SIMPLIFIED FORM	PRESENT MEANING
 𩵋	角	角	horn, corner, angle

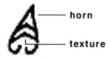

— horn

— texture

'𩵋' looks like a horn of an animal with texture on the surface.
The word is a pictograph of a horn.

THE PROGRESSION OF THE ANCIENT CHARACTER TO PRESENT CHARACTER   **PRONUNCIATION**

jiǎo

中國文字

76

ANCIENT CHARACTER	PRESENT FORM	SIMPLIFIED FORM	PRESENT MEANING
爪爪	爪	爪	claw, talon

'爪爪' looks like a pair of paws with sharp claws.
The word is a pictograph.

THE PROGRESSION OF THE ANCIENT CHARACTER TO PRESENT CHARACTER	PRONUNCIATION
爪 爪 爪 爪爪 爪 爪 爪	zhǎo

77

ANCIENT CHARACTER	PRESENT FORM	SIMPLIFIED FORM	PRESENT MEANING
飛	飛	飞	fly, hover or flutter in the air

head of bird
feather in the neck
body
wings

The word looks like a bird flying with both wings flapping in the wind. It is a pictograph.

THE PROGRESSION OF THE ANCIENT CHARACTER TO PRESENT CHARACTER | PRONUNCIATION

𡗎	𣆍	飛	飛	fēi

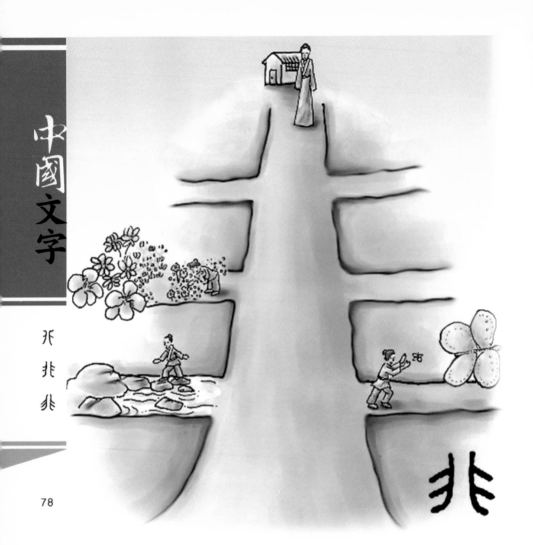

非
非
非

78

ANCIENT CHARACTER	PRESENT FORM	SIMPLIFIED FORM	PRESENT MEANING
非	非	非	wrong, wrong doing, evildoing, not, no

both the two wings and their feathers are arranged in opposite directions

The feathers of two wings are arranged in different directions when a bird is soaring. It implies difference, and contradiction in value.

THE PROGRESSION OF THE ANCIENT CHARACTER TO PRESENT CHARACTER   PRONUNCIATION

非 非 非 非   fēi

中國文字

東
巢
巢

ANCIENT CHARACTER	PRESENT FORM	SIMPLIFIED FORM	PRESENT MEANING
巢	巢	巢	nest

birds
nest
tree

It is a pictograph: '巢' looks like birds in their nest of a tree.

THE PROGRESSION OF THE ANCIENT CHARACTER TO PRESENT CHARACTER | PRONUNCIATION

| 東 巢 巢 巢 | cháo |

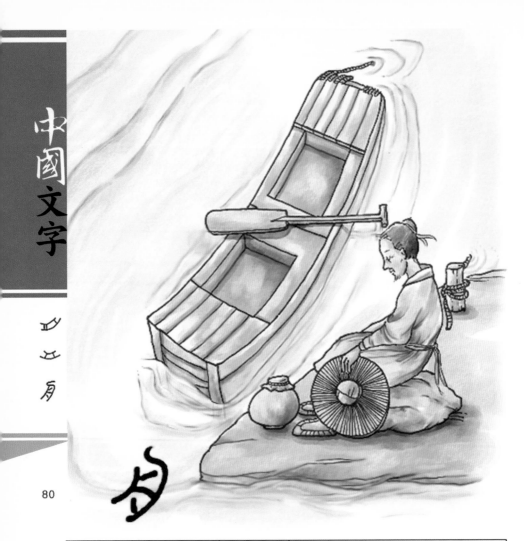

ANCIENT CHARACTER	PRESENT FORM	SIMPLIFIED FORM	PRESENT MEANING
舟	舟	舟	boat

'舟' is a pictograph. It looks like a small two-seat boat anchored by the riverbank.

THE PROGRESSION OF THE ANCIENT CHARACTER TO PRESENT CHARACTER	PRONUNCIATION
凵 月 皿 凵 月 月 月 舟	zhōu

車

ANCIENT CHARACTER	PRESENT FORM	SIMPLIFIED FORM	PRESENT MEANING
車	車	车	vehicle

- wheel
- body of the vehicle
- axle
- wheel

The word is a pictograph: '車' is the top view of a cart.

THE PROGRESSION OF THE ANCIENT CHARACTER TO PRESENT CHARACTER	PRONUNCIATION
輷 車 畖 輨 車 車 輚 車 車	chē

ANCIENT CHARACTER	PRESENT FORM	SIMPLIFIED FORM	PRESENT MEANING
网	網	网	net

It is a pictograph: '网' is a net knitted with cross pattern.

网 — net
　 — pattern

网 — net
　 — sound of the word

网 — net
　 — silk/linen (material)

THE PROGRESSION OF THE ANCIENT CHARACTER TO PRESENT CHARACTER | PRONUNCIATION

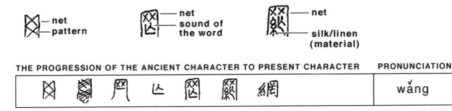

wǎng

ANCIENT CHARACTER	PRESENT FORM	SIMPLIFIED FORM	PRESENT MEANING
傘	傘	伞	umbrella

— veil —
— hanger —
— handle —

'傘' is a pictograph.
It is a picture of an umbrella.

THE PROGRESSION OF THE ANCIENT CHARACTER TO PRESENT CHARACTER | PRONUNCIATION

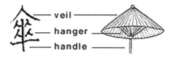

| 傘 | sǎn |

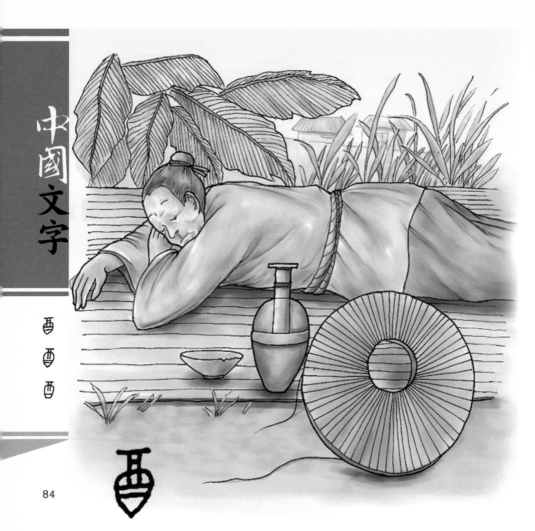

84

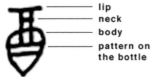

ANCIENT CHARACTER	PRESENT FORM	SIMPLIFIED FORM	PRESENT MEANING
酉	酉	酉	'酉' is seldom used. Words containing it relate to wine: '酒 wine', '酌 drink wine', '酊 drunk', '酗 alcoholic'

lip
neck
body
pattern on the bottle

'酉' looks like a bottle with a lip, neck, body and pattern on it.
It is a pictograph of a wine bottle.
Words containing '酉' relate to wine.

THE PROGRESSION OF THE ANCIENT CHARACTER TO PRESENT CHARACTER | PRONUNCIATION

| 酉 酉 酉 酉 酉 | yǒu |

ANCIENT CHARACTER	PRESENT FORM	SIMPLIFIED FORM	PRESENT MEANING
	筆		pen

— hand

— pen

It is a pictograph: '　' looks like a hand holding a pen. It meant 'pen' in ancient times. Later, '竹 bamboo' was added to the top of the word to indicate the material that the pen was made of.

THE PROGRESSION OF THE ANCIENT CHARACTER TO PRESENT CHARACTER   PRONUNCIATION

		bǐ

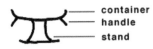

86

ANCIENT CHARACTER	PRESENT FORM	SIMPLIFIED FORM	PRESENT MEANING
皿	皿	皿	container

container
handle
stand

It is a pictograph: '皿' is a picture of a container.

THE PROGRESSION OF THE ANCIENT CHARACTER TO PRESENT CHARACTER | PRONUNCIATION

皿　皿	mǐn

ANCIENT CHARACTER	PRESENT FORM	SIMPLIFIED FORM	PRESENT MEANING
缶	缶	缶	ceramic container

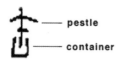

— pestle
— container

It is a pictograph. '缶' is a ceramic container used to hold wine or water. The big one served as a bottle while the small one could be used as a cup. The pestle might be used to crush ingredients for making wine. Words combined with '缶' relate to ceramic products.

THE PROGRESSION OF THE ANCIENT CHARACTER TO PRESENT CHARACTER PRONUNCIATION

	PRONUNCIATION
缶 缶 缶 缶 缶	fǒu

中國文字

ANCIENT CHARACTER	PRESENT FORM	SIMPLIFIED FORM	PRESENT MEANING
孑	斗	斗	a unit (1 decaliter) of dry measure for grain

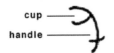

It is a pictograph: '孑' is a container with a handle which was used to measure volume. It was also a unit of volume in olden times.

THE PROGRESSION OF THE ANCIENT CHARACTER TO PRESENT CHARACTER | PRONUNCIATION

| 孑 孑 孓 考 斗 | dǒu |

中國文字

89

ANCIENT CHARACTER	PRESENT FORM	SIMPLIFIED FORM	PRESENT MEANING
豆	豆	豆	peas, beans

— cover
— container
— stand

light —

oil lamp —

'豆' is a pictograph of a container for food. In ancient China the oil lamp, which was shaped like a '豆', was also called '豆'. Moreover, the small dim light emitted from the lamp's wick looked like a bean or pea. The people then also called bean and pea '豆'. ('豆 bean/pea' is a borrowed.)

Borrowed: New word is formed with its own meaning by borrowing other word that has a similar pronunciation.

THE PROGRESSION OF THE ANCIENT CHARACTER TO PRESENT CHARACTER

PRONUNCIATION

| 豆 豆 豆 豆 豆 豆 豆 豆 | dòu |

工

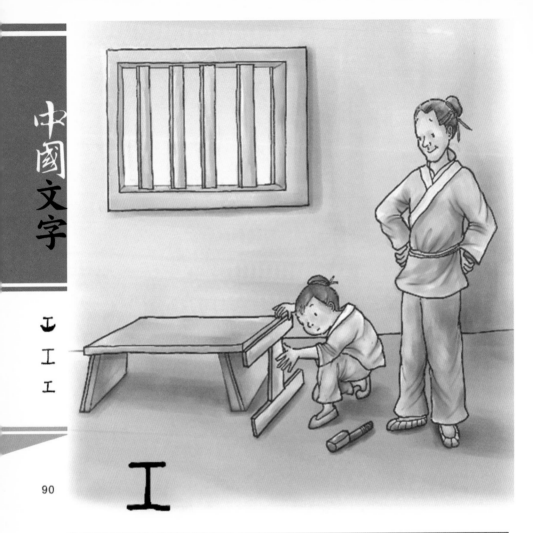

工

ANCIENT CHARACTER	PRESENT FORM	SIMPLIFIED FORM	PRESENT MEANING
工	工	工	worker, work, the working class

'工' was the ruler used for measurement in carpentry. The word is a pictograph of a ruler.

THE PROGRESSION OF THE ANCIENT CHARACTER TO PRESENT CHARACTER	PRONUNCIATION
工 工 工	gōng

ANCIENT CHARACTER	PRESENT FORM	SIMPLIFIED FORM	PRESENT MEANING
刀	刀	刀	knife, sword

'刀' is a picture of a knife. The word is a pictograph.

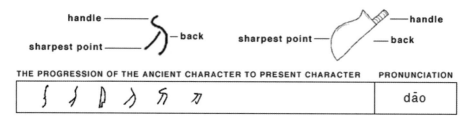

handle — back

sharpest point —

sharpest point — handle — back

THE PROGRESSION OF THE ANCIENT CHARACTER TO PRESENT CHARACTER

PRONUNCIATION

dāo

92

ANCIENT CHARACTER	PRESENT FORM	SIMPLIFIED FORM	PRESENT MEANING
斤	斤	斤	It is a unit of weight: 1 斤 = 1/2 kilogram

— axe with sharp blade

— axe the motion of operating an axe

'斤' is a pictograph of an axe which was used for chopping wood in ancient time.

THE PROGRESSION OF THE ANCIENT CHARACTER TO PRESENT CHARACTER | PRONUNCIATION

THE PROGRESSION OF THE ANCIENT CHARACTER TO PRESENT CHARACTER	PRONUNCIATION
斤 斤 斤 斤 斤 斤 斤 斤 斤 斤 斤	jīn

ANCIENT CHARACTER	PRESENT FORM	SIMPLIFIED FORM	PRESENT MEANING
 𠂔 𠂔	矢	矢	arrow

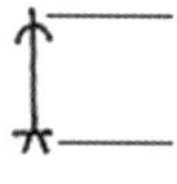

— pointed head of arrow
— feather attached at the end

It is a pictograph: '𠂔' is a picture of an arrow.

THE PROGRESSION OF THE ANCIENT CHARACTER TO PRESENT CHARACTER	PRONUNCIATION
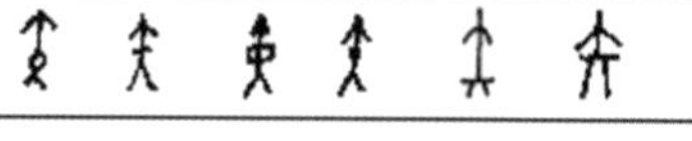 𠂔 𠂔 𠂔 𠂔 𠂔 𠂔 矢	shǐ

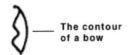

中國文字

ANCIENT CHARACTER	PRESENT FORM	SIMPLIFIED FORM	PRESENT MEANING
弓	弓	弓	bow, bend, arch

弓 —— The contour of a bow

It is a pictograph: '弓' looks like a bow. It was a weapon that the ancient Chinese used for shooting arrows when they went hunting or fought.

THE PROGRESSION OF THE ANCIENT CHARACTER TO PRESENT CHARACTER

	PRONUNCIATION
弓 弓 弓 弓 弓 弓	gōng

ANCIENT CHARACTER	PRESENT FORM	SIMPLIFIED FORM	PRESENT MEANING
𠎷	戈	戈	dagger-axe

The word is a pictograph: '𠎷' is a weapon with a long handle and a knife on one end. Words containing '𠎷' may mean weapons or doing something by using weapons. e.g. '國 kingdom', and '成 success'.

THE PROGRESSION OF THE ANCIENT CHARACTER TO PRESENT CHARACTER | PRONUNCIATION
| 𠎷 𢦏 于 槑 戈 戔 戈 | gē |

ANCIENT CHARACTER	PRESENT FORM	SIMPLIFIED FORM	PRESENT MEANING
𡳿	至	至	to, until, reach, arrive

The word is a pictograph. '𡳿' means ground, ' 𐓊 ' means arrow. An arrow is stuck into the ground. It implies something or someone has arrived.

THE PROGRESSION OF THE ANCIENT CHARACTER TO PRESENT CHARACTER | PRONUNCIATION

					至	zhì

中國文字

ANCIENT CHARACTER	PRESENT FORM	SIMPLIFIED FORM	PRESENT MEANING
	吉	吉	lucky, auspicious, propitious

— weapon
— shelf

It is a pictograph: ' ' is a picture showing weapons on a shelf.
A peaceful time is when weapons are being stored.

THE PROGRESSION OF THE ANCIENT CHARACTER TO PRESENT CHARACTER	PRONUNCIATION
	jí

巾 巾 巾

巾

ANCIENT CHARACTER	PRESENT FORM	SIMPLIFIED FORM	PRESENT MEANING
巾	巾	巾	a piece of cloth - as used for a towel, scarf, kerchief

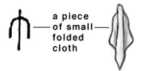

a piece of small folded cloth

It is a pictograph: '巾' is like a small piece of folded cloth hanging on a hook or lying on a man's shoulder. Words containing '巾' relate to items made out of cloth, for example '帽 hat'.

THE PROGRESSION OF THE ANCIENT CHARACTER TO PRESENT CHARACTER | PRONUNCIATION

| 巾 巾 巾 巾 | jīn |

ANCIENT CHARACTER	PRESENT FORM	SIMPLIFIED FORM	PRESENT MEANING
絲	絲	丝	silk

— a bundle of silk —

It is a pictograph: '絲' looks like threads of silk tied together as a bundle.

THE PROGRESSION OF THE ANCIENT CHARACTER TO PRESENT CHARACTER | PRONUNCIATION
sī

ANCIENT CHARACTER	PRESENT FORM	SIMPLIFIED FORM	PRESENT MEANING
㐭	衣	衣	clothing, clothes, garment, a coating

collar
shoulder
right part of the clothing covers the left part

It is a pictograph that shows the clothing for the upper part of the body of the ancient Chinese.

THE PROGRESSION OF THE ANCIENT CHARACTER TO PRESENT CHARACTER

PRONUNCIATION

yī

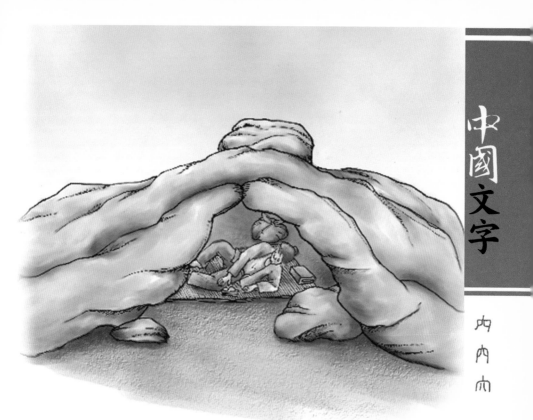

內 內 朮

101

ANCIENT CHARACTER	PRESENT FORM	SIMPLIFIED FORM	PRESENT MEANING
朮	穴	穴	cave, den

 hill / cave
— opening

It is a pictograph: '朮' looks like a cave with an opening. Caves used to be the homes of some people in ancient times.

THE PROGRESSION OF THE ANCIENT CHARACTER TO PRESENT CHARACTER | PRONUNCIATION

| 內 內 朮 穴 | xué |

102

ANCIENT CHARACTER	PRESENT FORM	SIMPLIFIED FORM	PRESENT MEANING
囪	窗	窗	window

It is a pictograph: '囪' is a picture of a window.
Later, ' 宀 cave/dwelling' is added on the top of the word
indicating that the window is inside of a cave/dwelling.

THE PROGRESSION OF THE ANCIENT CHARACTER TO PRESENT CHARACTER | PRONUNCIATION

							chuāng

ANCIENT CHARACTER	PRESENT FORM	SIMPLIFIED FORM	PRESENT MEANING
戶	戸	户	door, a household

— door with one panel
— wood strip

It is a pictograph: '戶' looks like a door with one panel, and a wood strip across it.

THE PROGRESSION OF THE ANCIENT CHARACTER TO PRESENT CHARACTER	PRONUNCIATION
戶 戸 戶 户	hù

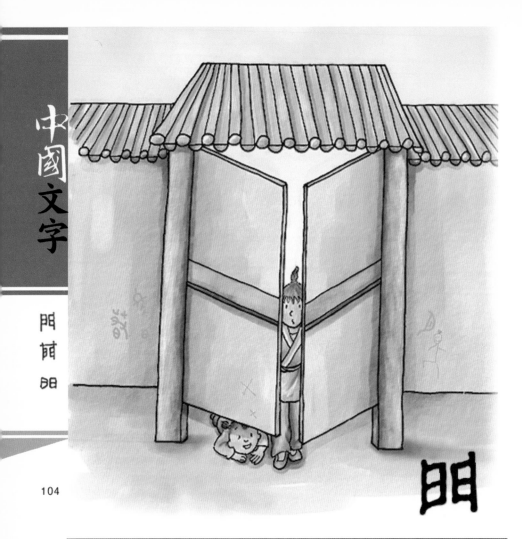

ANCIENT CHARACTER	PRESENT FORM	SIMPLIFIED FORM	PRESENT MEANING
門	門	门	door, gate

門 — a frame of '日'

It is a pictograph: '門' is a picture of a door consisting of two pieces of wood or two frames of ' 日 '.

THE PROGRESSION OF THE ANCIENT CHARACTER TO PRESENT CHARACTER	PRONUNCIATION
門 門 門 門 門 門	mén

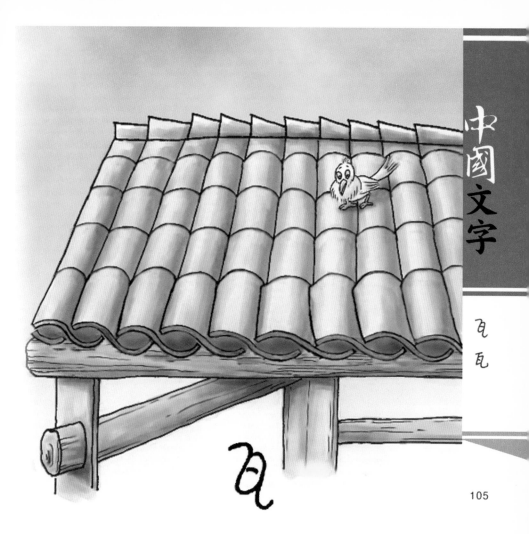

瓦
瓦

105

ANCIENT CHARACTER	PRESENT FORM	SIMPLIFIED FORM	PRESENT MEANING
瓦	瓦	瓦	tile

～	The arrangement of tiles
瓦	The comparision of the drawing and the word

It is a pictograph: '瓦' looks like the vertical arrangement of two tiles. The dash may indicate the space between them. Words containing '瓦' mean things made out of tile or ceramic.

THE PROGRESSION OF THE ANCIENT CHARACTER TO PRESENT CHARACTER	PRONUNCIATION
瓦 瓦	wǎ

中國文字

ANCIENT CHARACTER	PRESENT FORM	SIMPLIFIED FORM	PRESENT MEANING
	西	西	west

— bird

— nest

Birds come back to their nests when the sun sets in the west. The word is a pictograph.

THE PROGRESSION OF THE ANCIENT CHARACTER TO PRESENT CHARACTER	PRONUNCIATION
西	xī

𝍖

坴

血

107

ANCIENT CHARACTER	PRESENT FORM	SIMPLIFIED FORM	PRESENT MEANING
𠂤	齊	齐	neat, even (in good order), on a level with

— grains of wheat

— lowland

It is a pictograph: The grains of wheat look like they are growing at the same level when viewed by the lowland.

THE PROGRESSION OF THE ANCIENT CHARACTER TO PRESENT CHARACTER

PRONUNCIATION

𝍖 𝍖 𝍖 𝍖𝍖 𝍖𝍖𝍖 齊 坴 血 𣥂 齊 齊	qí

入 入 入

108

ANCIENT CHARACTER	PRESENT FORM	SIMPLIFIED FORM	PRESENT MEANING
入	入	入	enter, join

It is a pictograph: '入' is like something on its way down from above.

THE PROGRESSION OF THE ANCIENT CHARACTER TO PRESENT CHARACTER	PRONUNCIATION
人 入 入 入 內 入	rù

ANCIENT CHARACTER	PRESENT FORM	SIMPLIFIED FORM	PRESENT MEANING
𠤱	付	付	give, pay, hand over to

'𠤱' combines with '亻 a person', and '寸 a hand holding something'.
A person is handing something to the other person.
It is an ideative.

Ideative: word formed from two words/signs which combine to suggest a new meaning.

THE PROGRESSION OF THE ANCIENT CHARACTER TO PRESENT CHARACTER   PRONUNCIATION

𠤱 付 付	fù

ANCIENT CHARACTER	PRESENT FORM	SIMPLIFIED FORM	PRESENT MEANING
休	休	休	stop, cease, end, rest

'休' combines '亻person', '朩 tree'.
A man rests by leaning on a tree. It is an ideative.

THE PROGRESSION OF THE ANCIENT CHARACTER TO PRESENT CHARACTER   PRONUNCIATION

休 休 休 休 休	xiū

ANCIENT CHARACTER	PRESENT FORM	SIMPLIFIED FORM	PRESENT MEANING
大	立	立	stand, erect, set up

'立' combines ' 大 big/a person', ' — ground'.
A person stands on the ground with both hands stretching out.
Its original meaning was 'stand'.
The word is an ideative.

THE PROGRESSION OF THE ANCIENT CHARACTER TO PRESENT CHARACTER | PRONUNCIATION

| 大 大 大 企 立 立 立 | lì |

ANCIENT CHARACTER	PRESENT FORM	SIMPLIFIED FORM	PRESENT MEANING
竝	位	位	place, location, site, seat

' 竝 combines ' 丿 a person', '立 stand'.
A person stands on the ground -- he takes up some space.
Its original meaning was 'position'. The word is an ideative.

THE PROGRESSION OF THE ANCIENT CHARACTER TO PRESENT CHARACTER | PRONUNCIATION

| 立 亻 竝 位 位 位 | wèi |

中國文字

113

ANCIENT CHARACTER	PRESENT FORM	SIMPLIFIED FORM	PRESENT MEANING
𧙃	依	依	depend on, listen to(advice), according to

It is a fetus in its mother's womb. A fetus relies completely on its mother. Its original meaning was 'depend on'.

'衣 clothes' is used in this word as embryonic membrane. *(p.100)*

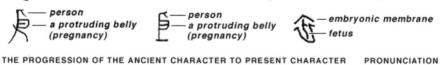

身 — person — a protruding belly (pregnancy)

𦣻 — person — a protruding belly (pregnancy)

𧙃 — embryonic membrane — fetus

THE PROGRESSION OF THE ANCIENT CHARACTER TO PRESENT CHARACTER | PRONUNCIATION

身 𦣻 𧙃 𠆳 㑄 依	yī

中國文字

ANCIENT CHARACTER	PRESENT FORM	SIMPLIFIED FORM	PRESENT MEANING
[illegible]	信	信	confidence, trust, faith, a letter

It is an ideative: it combines '亻 person' and '言 saying'. What a person says is his promise.

THE PROGRESSION OF THE ANCIENT CHARACTER TO PRESENT CHARACTER	PRONUNCIATION
[illegible] [illegible] [illegible] 信	xìn

115

ANCIENT CHARACTER	PRESENT FORM	SIMPLIFIED FORM	PRESENT MEANING
㑣	保	保	protect, defend, keep, maintain, preserve

It is an ideative: The word combines '亻 person' and '孚 child'. A person carrying a child on his back. Its orginal meaning was 'protect'.

THE PROGRESSION OF THE ANCIENT CHARACTER TO PRESENT CHARACTER | PURONUNCIATION

| 㑣 㑣 㑣 保 保 保 | bǎo |

116

ANCIENT CHARACTER	PRESENT FORM	SIMPLIFIED FORM	PRESENT MEANING
㲃	伏	伏	bend over, lie prostrate, subside, go down

The word combines ' 亻 person' and ' 犬 dog'.
The person's posture is like a dog crawling or creeping on the ground as if he is trying to hide from somebody or hunt for something. It is an ideative.

THE PROGRESSION OF THE ANCIENT CHARACTER TO PRESENT CHARACTER | **PRONUNCIATION**

㲃 㲃 㲃 伏	fú

ANCIENT CHARACTER	PRESENT FORM	SIMPLIFIED FORM	PRESENT MEANING
𠤎𠤎	比	比	compare, compete

The word combines ' 𠤎 person', and ' 𠤎 person'.
Two people are very close to each other.
Its original meaning was 'intimate'. It is an ideative.

THE PROGRESSION OF THE ANCIENT CHARACTER TO PRESENT CHARACTER

	PRONUNCIATION
𠤎𠤎 𠤎𠤎 𠤎𠤎 𠤎𠤎 从 比 𠤎𠤎 从 比	bǐ

中國文字

仌 仌 仌

118

ANCIENT CHARACTER	PRESENT FORM	SIMPLIFIED FORM	PRESENT MEANING
仌	北	北	north

仌 —— person

The word combines two people standing back to back. It shows the coldness between them. Its original meaning was 'difference', and also the coldest region in China -- the north.

THE PROGRESSION OF THE ANCIENT CHARACTER TO PRESENT CHARACTER   PRONUNCIATION

仌 仌 仌 北 北	běi

竹
竹
从

119

ANCIENT CHARACTER	PRESENT FORM	SIMPLIFIED FORM	PRESENT MEANING
竹	從	从	follow, obey

竹 — person
— person

The word combines two persons together. A person behind follows the person in front of him. Its original meaning was 'follows'. It is an ideative.

THE PROGRESSION OF THE ANCIENT CHARACTER TO PRESENT CHARACTER   **PRONUNCIATION**

竹 竹 从	cóng

ANCIENT CHARACTER	PRESENT FORM	SIMPLIFIED FORM	PRESENT MEANING
	眾	从	many, numerous, crowd, multitude

sun

people

The word combines ' ⊖ the sun', ' 'ᴼᴼᴼ three people', three symbolizes a number of. There are a number of people out there under the sun. Its original meaning was 'many people'. The word is an ideative.

some ancient words: ' 日 the sun' was also written as 'ᵈ'.

THE PROGRESSION OF THE ANCIENT CHARACTER TO PRESENT CHARACTER   **PRONUNCIATION**

	zhòng

ANCIENT CHARACTER	PRESENT FORM	SIMPLIFIED FORM	PRESENT MEANING
㞢卪	此	此	this, here, this place

person
foot

person
foot

'㞢卪' combines '㞢 foot/proceed', and '卪 a person points to the ground'. The word shows that a person proceeds until he reaches his destination: the person points to the ground to mean that it is 'right here'. Its original meaning was 'stop'. By extension to the place where a person stops, it also meant 'right there'.

THE PROGRESSION OF THE ANCIENT CHARACTER TO PRESENT CHARACTER   PRONUNCIATION

㞢卪 㞢卪 㞢卪 㞢卪 此 此 此	cǐ

ANCIENT CHARACTER	PRESENT FORM	SIMPLIFIED FORM	PRESENT MEANING
𣦵	死	死	die, dead

'𣦵' combines '歺 dry bone or corpse', '𠤎 a person'.
A person is mourning over the dead. It shows immense sadness.
Its original meaning was 'dead'.
The word is an ideative.

THE PROGRESSION OF THE ANCIENT CHARACTER TO PRESENT CHARACTER   PRONUNCIATION

𣦵 𣦵 𣦵 死	sǐ

ANCIENT CHARACTER	PRESENT FORM	SIMPLIFIED FORM	PRESENT MEANING
葬	葬	葬	bury

—— grass
—— the dead
—— cloth/mat
—— grass

'葬' combines '艸 grass', '死 the dead'.
The dead was laid on the grass, and covered
by a layer of grass. It was the custom to bury
the dead in the wilderness in olden times.
It is an ideative.

THE PROGRESSION OF THE ANCIENT CHARACTER TO PRESENT CHARACTER | PRONUNCIATION

葬 葬 葬 葬 葬	zàng

ANCIENT CHARACTER	PRESENT FORM	SIMPLIFIED FORM	PRESENT MEANING
天	天	天	the sky, heaven, day, a period of time in a day

'天' combines ' 一 the sky', and ' 大 big or person'.
The man is so tall that he almost reaches the sky. Or the sky
is on the top of a person's head. The word is an ideative.

THE PROGRESSION OF THE ANCIENT CHARACTER TO PRESENT CHARACTER   PRONUNCIATION

朿 天 夭 页 天 天	tiān

125

ANCIENT CHARACTER	PRESENT FORM	SIMPLIFIED FORM	PRESENT MEANING
文	文	文	writing

'文' is a person with a tattoo on his chest. The beautiful line work and contour of the tattoo reflect a kind of culture. '文' meant picture with overlapping line work and texture, and also the pictographs of the Chinese words.

'文', therefore, relates to writing and words, such as '文章 passage or essay', and '文化 culture'.

THE PROGRESSION OF THE ANCIENT CHARACTER TO PRESENT CHARACTER

文　文　文　文　文　文	PRONUNCIATION
	wén

ANCIENT CHARACTER	PRESENT FORM	SIMPLIFIED FORM	PRESENT MEANING
	鬥	斗	fight, tussle

'鬥' is like two people fighting fiercely so that they twist each others faces.

'鬥' is like two people all tangled up in a fight.

- person
- hand

- hand
- person

THE PROGRESSION OF THE ANCIENT CHARACTER TO PRESENT CHARACTER | PRONUNCIATION

| | dòu |

ANCIENT CHARACTER	PRESENT FORM	SIMPLIFIED FORM	PRESENT MEANING
色	色	色	color, countenance, look

'色' contains two people. One is sitting on his knee '巴' while the other is standing '勹' beside him. The standing person seems to be observing the other person. Its original meaning was 'countenance'.

THE PROGRESSION OF THE ANCIENT CHARACTER TO PRESENT CHARACTER	PRONUNCIATION
色 色	sè

ANCIENT CHARACTER	PRESENT FORM	SIMPLIFIED FORM	PRESENT MEANING
到	到	到	arrive, leave for

arrow
person
soil

'到' combines '至 an arrow stuck to the ground', and ' 人 a person'. A person collects an arrow which may carry a message. Its original meaning was 'arrive'. It is a ideative.

THE PROGRESSION OF THE ANCIENT CHARACTER TO PRESENT CHARACTER   PRONUNCIATION

到　到　到　位　到　到　到   dào

129

ANCIENT CHARACTER	PRESENT FORM	SIMPLIFIED FORM	PRESENT MEANING
歬	前	前	front, forward, ahead, before

'止 feet' symbolizes moving forward.
'歬' shows an advancing boat with a passenger.
It illustrates the state of proceeding. Its original meaning was 'moving forward.'
It is an ideative.

proceed —
person —
boat —

THE PROGRESSION OF THE ANCIENT CHARACTER TO PRESENT CHARACTER   PRONUNCIATION

qián

130

ANCIENT CHARACTER	PRESENT FORM	SIMPLIFIED FORM	PRESENT MEANING
皀卩	即	即	be near, soon, reach, approach

'皀卩' combines ' 皀 a food container', and ' 卩 a sitter'.
A person sitting near a food container implies that the food is soon
be ready. Its original meaning was 'to bend down to eat' which
implies approaching. The word is an ideative.

THE PROGRESSION OF THE ANCIENT CHARACTER TO PRESENT CHARACTER	PRONUNCIATION
皀卩 皀卩 皀卩 皀卩 皀卩 卽 即	jí

ANCIENT CHARACTER	PRESENT FORM	SIMPLIFIED FORM	PRESENT MEANING
忄坐	性	性	character, disposition, quality, sex

'忄坐' combines '忄 heart', and '坐 give birth to/come from'.
One's character comes from one's own heart. Its original meaning
was 'the nature of a person'.
It is a harmonic and also an ideative. ('忄坐' takes the sound of '坐 ',
and a person's nature is from the '忄 heart').

*Harmonic: word fromed from two words/signs combine together; one stands for
its meaning, and the other stands for its pronunciation.*

THE PROGRESSION OF THE ANCIENT CHARACTER TO PRESENT CHARACTER   **PRONUNCIATION**

坐 忄坐 性	xìng

132

ANCIENT CHARACTER	PRESENT FORM	SIMPLIFIED FORM	PRESENT MEANING
	慈	慈	kind, loving, parental love, one's own mother

 — silk
      — heart

'' means kindness and love, specifically parental love. Parental love is like silk which is delicate but strong and seems never ending.

THE PROGRESSION OF THE ANCIENT CHARACTER TO PRESENT CHARACTER	PRONUNCIATION
慈 慈 慈	cí

133

ANCIENT CHARACTER	PRESENT FORM	SIMPLIFIED FORM	PRESENT MEANING
耳心	耳心	耻	shame, disgrace, humilation

'耳心' combines ' 耳 ear', and ' 心 heart'.
A person hears a bad comment about himself through the ear.
The comment reaches deep down to his heart. He feels ashamed of
himself.

THE PROGRESSION OF THE ANCIENT CHARACTER TO PRESENT CHARACTER	PRONUNCIATION
耳心 耳心	chǐ

中國文字

ANCIENT CHARACTER	PRESENT FORM	SIMPLIFIED FORM	PRESENT MEANING
恆	恆	恒	permanent, lasting, perseverance

heart(symbol of resolution)
— moon
— symbol of continuity

When one makes a decision in one's heart, one shall abide by it. That is like the moon which will never fail to rise every night in the sky. Its original meaning was 'always'. The word is an ideative.

THE PROGRESSION OF THE ANCIENT CHARACTER TO PRESENT CHARACTER   **PRONUNCIATION**

恆 恆 恆 恆 恆	héng

ANCIENT CHARACTER	PRESENT FORM	SIMPLIFIED FORM	PRESENT MEANING
	志	志	will, aspiration

— stop

— heart

A dream which stays in one's heart becomes a will. Its original meaning was 'a will'.

THE PROGRESSION OF THE ANCIENT CHARACTER TO PRESENT CHARACTER	PRONUNCIATION
志	zhì

中國文字

ANCIENT CHARACTER	PRESENT FORM	SIMPLIFIED FORM	PRESENT MEANING
	思	思	think, consider, deliberate, think of

 —— brain

—— heart

The ancient Chinese thought that the brain and the heart were the two organs for thinking. The brain was for analysis while the heart was for passion and decision making -- the conscience. It is an ideative.

THE PROGRESSION OF THE ANCIENT CHARACTER TO PRESENT CHARACTER

PRONUNCIATION

思	sī

137

ANCIENT CHARACTER	PRESENT FORM	SIMPLIFIED FORM	PRESENT MEANING
	射	射	shoot

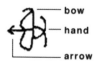

— bow
— hand
— arrow

A hand is holding a bow and an arrow.
The arrow is ready to be shot.
The word is an ideative.

THE PROGRESSION OF THE ANCIENT CHARACTER TO PRESENT CHARACTER   **PRONUNCIATION**

	shè

138

ANCIENT CHARACTER	PRESENT FORM	SIMPLIFIED FORM	PRESENT MEANING
𠬝	友	友	friend, friendly

𠂇 —— hand
𠂇 —— hand

The hands of two persons reach out together for something - a person offers help to another. They are friends.
It is an ideative.

THE PROGRESSION OF THE ANCIENT CHARACTER TO PRESENT CHARACTER | PRONUNCIATION

yǒu

ANCIENT CHARACTER	PRESENT FORM	SIMPLIFIED FORM	PRESENT MEANING
𠂆	失	失	lose, let slip

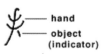
— hand
— object (indicator)

Something slips out of a person's hand and is going to be lost.
The word is an indicative.

Indicative: Indicator is added to a word/sign for telling things that cannot be drawn, like directions, positions, and numbers.

THE PROGRESSION OF THE ANCIENT CHARACTER TO PRESENT CHARACTER   PRONUNCIATION

𠂆 𠂆 失	shī

中國文字

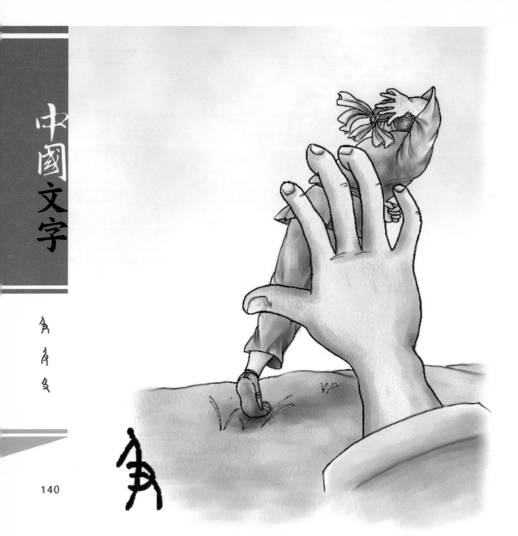

ANCIENT CHARACTER	PRESENT FORM	SIMPLIFIED FORM	PRESENT MEANING
	及	及	reach, come up to, in time for, and

—— person
—— hand

A person's hand reaches to another person.
Its original meaning was 'catch up'.
The word is an ideative.

THE PROGRESSION OF THE ANCIENT CHARACTER TO PRESENT CHARACTER | PRONUNCIATION

| | | | | jí |

ANCIENT CHARACTER	PRESENT FORM	SIMPLIFIED FORM	PRESENT MEANING
爭	爭	争	contend, strive, argue, dispute

— hand
— hand
— object

Two people with their hands grab for the same object. They are fighting for it. Words containing '爭' relate to fight. It is an ideative.

THE PROGRESSION OF THE ANCIENT CHARACTER TO PRESENT CHARACTER	PRONUNCIATION
爭 爭 爭 爭 争	zhēng

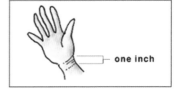

one inch

ANCIENT CHARACTER	PRESENT FORM	SIMPLIFIED FORM	PRESENT MEANING
寻	寸	寸	a unit of length (an inch), very little, short

The area just below the palm where the pulse is felt. The distance from the palm to the pulse is an inch. ' 习 ' is a hand, ' - ' is an indicator which tells the position of the pulse just below the hand. It is an indicative.

THE PROGRESSION OF THE ANCIENT CHARACTER TO PRESENT CHARACTER　　PRONUNCIATION

习 乡 寸	cùn

143

ANCIENT CHARACTER	PRESENT FORM	SIMPLIFIED FORM	PRESENT MEANING
爯	受	受	accept

object — hand

A person offers an object by hand, and the other person accepts it. The word is an ideative.

THE PROGRESSION OF THE ANCIENT CHARACTER TO PRESENT CHARACTER | PRONUNCIATION

爯 爭 爲 受	shòu

144

ANCIENT CHARACTER	PRESENT FORM	SIMPLIFIED FORM	PRESENT MEANING
㤅	愛	爱	love, affaction

— hand
— heart
— hand

'㤅' was formed from '旡'. A heart was added in the center of the word. One offers and the other accepts, both of them are with sincerity. The word is an ideative.

THE PROGRESSION OF THE ANCIENT CHARACTER TO PRESENT CHARACTER | PRONUNCIATION

					ài

捉
捉

145

捉

ANCIENT CHARACTER	PRESENT FORM	SIMPLIFIED FORM	PRESENT MEANING
捉	捉	捉	clutch, hold, grasp, catch, capture

'捉' combines '扌 hand', and '足 feet'.
If a person wants to catch something, one uses both one's hands and feet.

THE PROGRESSION OF THE ANCIENT CHARACTER TO PRESENT CHARACTER	PRONUNCIATION
捉 捉	zhuŏ

粒拉

ANCIENT CHARACTER	PRESENT FORM	SIMPLIFIED FORM	PRESENT MEANING
粒	拉	拉	pull, draw, tug, drag

粒 — hand
— a standing person

To pull by hand a person who stands on the ground.

THE PROGRESSION OF THE ANCIENT CHARACTER TO PRESENT CHARACTER | PRONUNCIATION

粒 拉 | lā

陷 阹 改

147

a student punishes himself for failing to recite a passage

ANCIENT CHARACTER	PRESENT FORM	SIMPLIFIED FORM	PRESENT MEANING
陷	改	改	change, revise, correct, put right

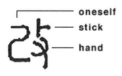

— oneself
— stick
— hand

A person makes a mistake, so he holds a stick with his hand and hits himself. This is to help him remember the mistake and improve upon himself.

THE PROGRESSION OF THE ANCIENT CHARACTER TO PRESENT CHARACTER | PRONUNCIATION

陷 阹 阹 改 改 | gǎi

ANCIENT CHARACTER	PRESENT FORM	SIMPLIFIED FORM	PRESENT MEANING
	奉	奉	give or present with respect

— an object
— hand

'奉' looks like two hands holding something upward for someone with respect. Its original meaning was 'offering with respect'.
'奉' takes the sound of '丰'.

THE PROGRESSION OF THE ANCIENT CHARACTER TO PRESENT CHARACTER   **PRONUNCIATION**

奉	fèng

ANCIENT CHARACTER	PRESENT FORM	SIMPLIFIED FORM	PRESENT MEANING
攴	父	父	father

— stick
— hand

'父' combines ' | a stick', and '手 hand'. A person holding a stick implies a person who maintains discipline in the family. He is typically the father.
The word is an ideative.

THE PROGRESSION OF THE ANCIENT CHARACTER TO PRESENT CHARACTER

	PRONUNCIATION
攴 攴 攴 攴 攴 父	fù

中國文字

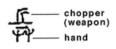

150

ANCIENT CHARACTER	PRESENT FORM	SIMPLIFIED FORM	PRESENT MEANING
	兵	兵	soldier, troops

— chopper (weapon)

— hand

'⟨character⟩' combines ' ⟨character⟩ weapon', and '⟨character⟩ two hands'. A person shows his weapon by holding it with his two hands -- he is a soldier. It is an ideative.

THE PROGRESSION OF THE ANCIENT CHARACTER TO PRESENT CHARACTER | PRONUNCIATION

bīng

鼓 鼓 鼓

151

ANCIENT CHARACTER	PRESENT FORM	SIMPLIFIED FORM	PRESENT MEANING
鼓	鼓	鼓	drum

decoration — 壴 — drumstick
drum — 鼓 — hand
stand

'鼓' combines ' 壴 drum', and
' 攴 a hand holding a drumstick'.
Its original meaning was 'to strike
a drum'. The word is an ideative.

THE PROGRESSION OF THE ANCIENT CHARACTER TO PRESENT CHARACTER	PRONUNCIATION
鼓 鼓 鼓 鼓	gǔ

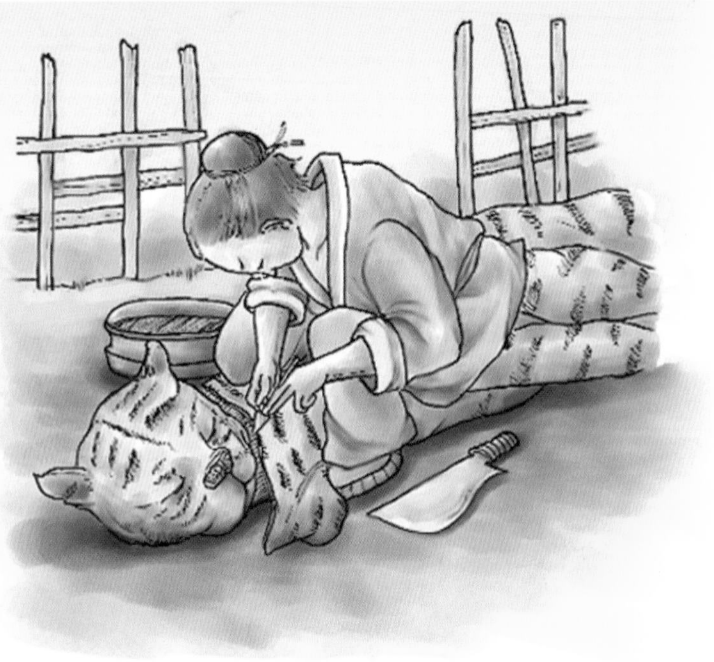

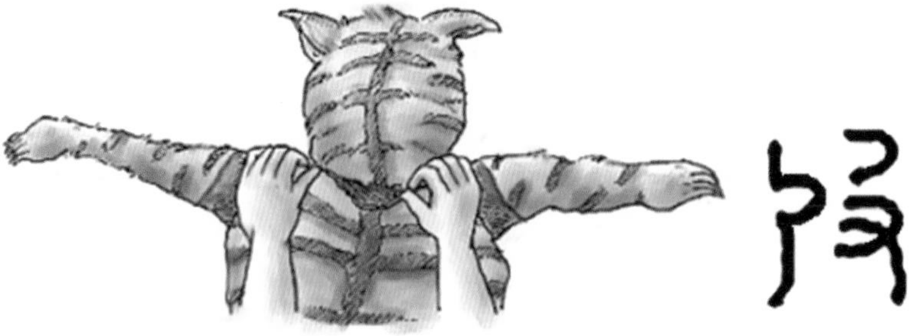

ANCIENT CHARACTER	PRESENT FORM	SIMPLIFIED FORM	PRESENT MEANING
[ancient character]	皮	皮	skin in general

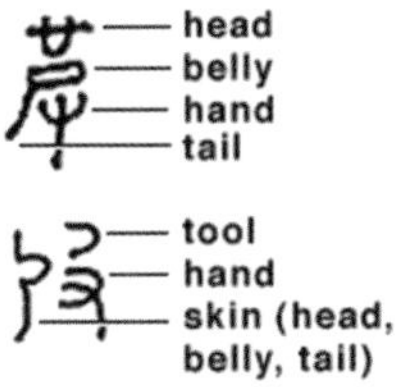
head
belly
hand
tail
tool
hand
skin (head, belly, tail)

'[ancient form]' shows the stripping of an animal skin. It emphasizes the head and the belly since stripping starts from the head, and the belly is the most useful part.

'[ancient form]', another word for 'animal skin' from later stage, shows how to get a piece of animal skin by using a tool. The word is an ideative.

THE PROGRESSION OF THE ANCIENT CHARACTER TO PRESENT CHARACTER	PRONUNCIATION
[ancient forms] 皮 皮	pí

革革革

153

ANCIENT CHARACTER	PRESENT FORM	SIMPLIFIED FORM	PRESENT MEANING
革	革	革	leather, hide

hand — 革 — animal skin with head and tail

'革' looks like two hands are working on a piece of animal skin. The original meaning of the word was 'a piece of treated animal skin'.

THE PROGRESSION OF THE ANCIENT CHARACTER TO PRESENT CHARACTER

革 革 革 革	PRONUNCIATION
	gé

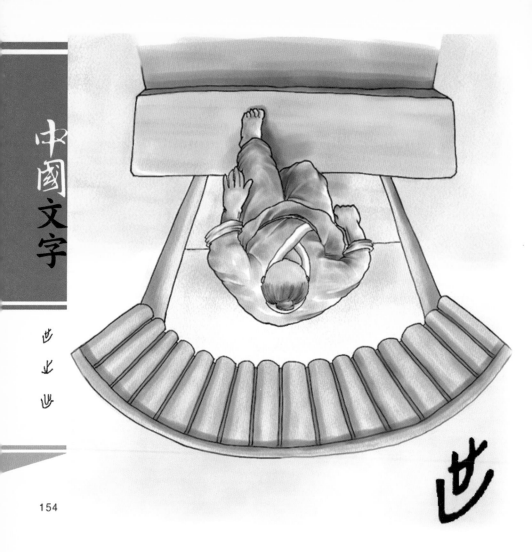

中國文字

154

ANCIENT CHARACTER	PRESENT FORM	SIMPLIFIED FORM	PRESENT MEANING
屮	出	出	go, come out, offer (money, advice, ideas)

 —— toes
—— dwelling

The feet of a person are stepping out from a dwelling -- he is going out. The word is an ideative.

THE PROGRESSION OF THE ANCIENT CHARACTER TO PRESENT CHARACTER | PRONUNCIATION

| 屮 屮 屮 屮 出 | chū |

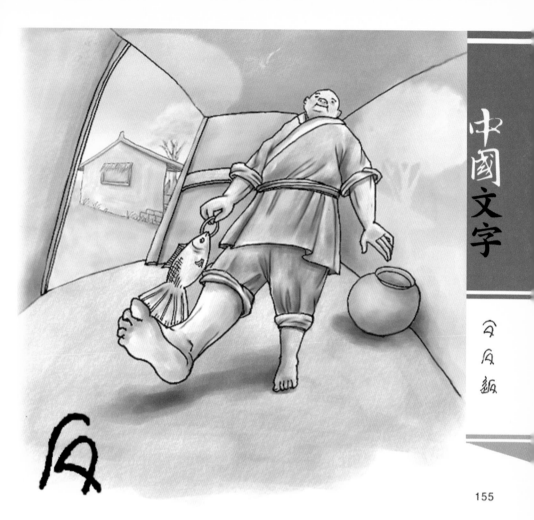

ANCIENT CHARACTER	PRESENT FORM	SIMPLIFIED FORM	PRESENT MEANING
反叛	返	返	return

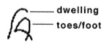
—— dwelling
—— toes/foot

A person returns to his dwelling with his toes '屮' pointing inside the house.
Later, '辵' (step by step) was added to the side of the word. It is an ideative.

THE PROGRESSION OF THE ANCIENT CHARACTER TO PRESENT CHARACTER ・ PRONUNCIATION

| 反 反 叛 返 | fǎn |

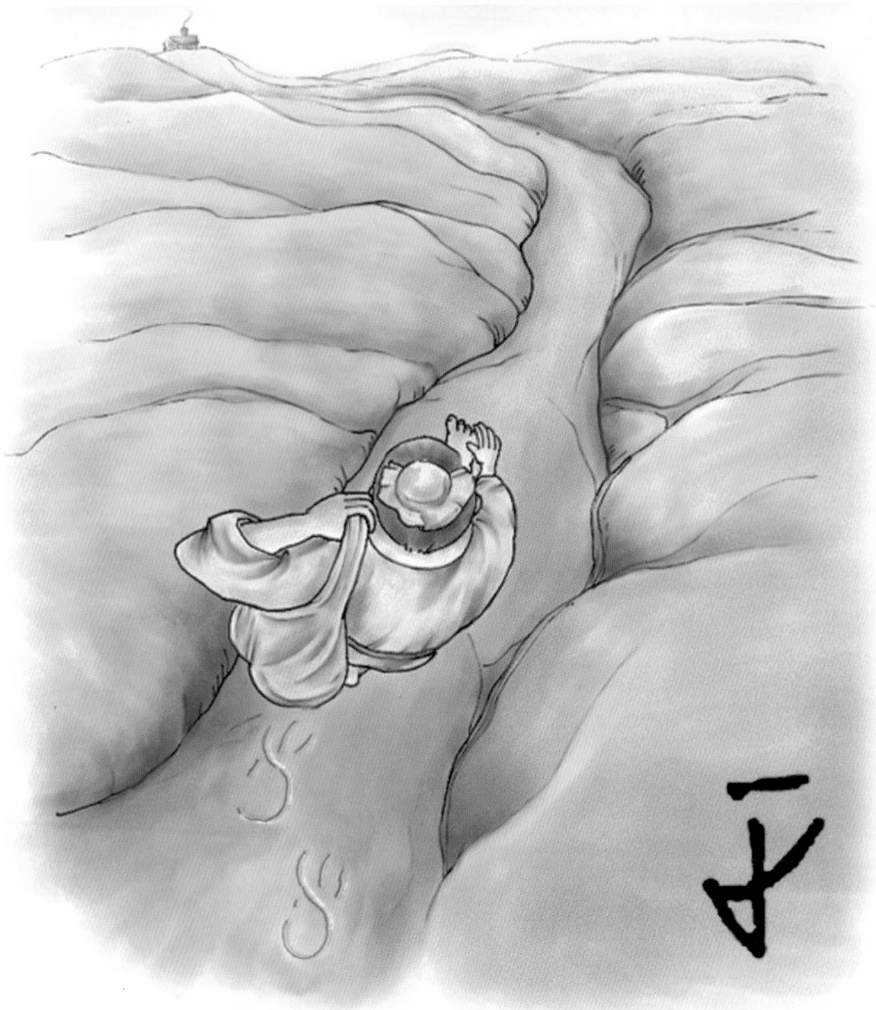

ANCIENT CHARACTER	PRESENT FORM	SIMPLIFIED FORM	PRESENT MEANING
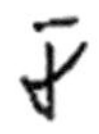	正	正	upright, correct, pure, precisely, situated in the middle, main

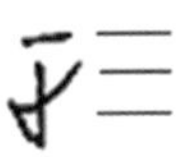

One should stay and stop where there is truth, justice and rightness. Its original meaning was: set off right to the destination, which implied a right decision.

When ' foot/toes' comes across an obstacle or destination ' ㅁ , – ' ,it stops there.

THE PROGRESSION OF THE ANCIENT CHARACTER TO PRESENT CHARACTER	PRONUNCIATION
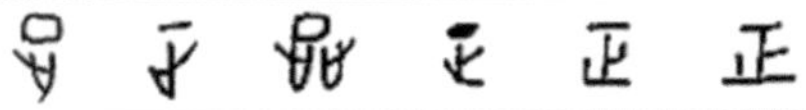	zhèng

是 是 是

ANCIENT CHARACTER	PRESENT FORM	SIMPLIFIED FORM	PRESENT MEANING
是	是	是	correct, right, this, that, yes, be

' 是 ' is at high noon with the sun exactly overhead. A person at this time stands under the sun. No shadow can be seen, but only a pair of his own feet. Everything then is exposed under the sun, nothing can be hidden. It implies 'righteousness'. As it is exactly at that moment when one doesn't see one's own shadow, it also means 'exactly' and 'this'.

THE PROGRESSION OF THE ANCIENT CHARACTER TO PRESENT CHARACTER	PRONUNCIATION
是 是 是 是 是	shì

ANCIENT CHARACTER	PRESENT FORM	SIMPLIFIED FORM	PRESENT MEANING
宀定	定	定	calm, stable

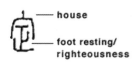
— house

— foot resting/ righteousness

When one's feet are at home (return home), one feels calm and safe.
Also, when righteousness lives in one's heart, one feels calm and safe.
The word illustrates the state of safety.
It is an ideative.

THE PROGRESSION OF THE ANCIENT CHARACTER TO PRESENT CHARACTER

	PRONUNCIATION
宀 宀 定 定 宀 定 定	dìng

走 态 走

159

ANCIENT CHARACTER	PRESENT FORM	SIMPLIFIED FORM	PRESENT MEANING
走	走	走	walk, go, run, move

It combines ' 大 like a person swinging his arms', and ' 止 feet'.
A person swinging his arms while his feet are moving. It illustrates
a person walking forward hurriedly. It is an ideative.

THE PROGRESSION OF THE ANCIENT CHARACTER TO PRESENT CHARACTER | PRONUNCIATION

| 走 态 走 走 | zǒu |

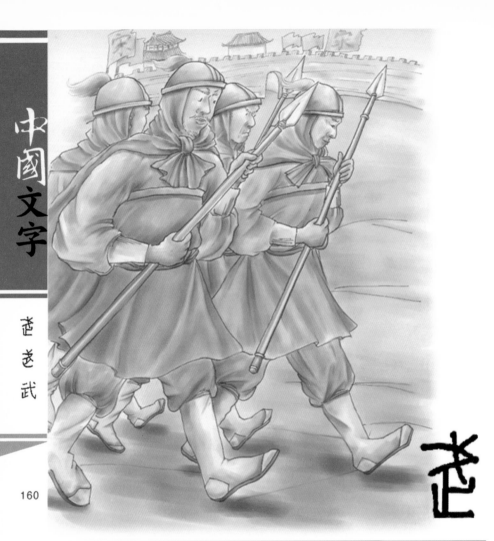

ANCIENT CHARACTER	PRESENT FORM	SIMPLIFIED FORM	PRESENT MEANING
走	武	武	force, use force

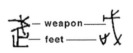

'走' combines '止 feet' which symbolizes action, and '戈 weapon'.
People/soldiers are armed with weapons and proceed -- war begins. Its original meaning was 'resort to force'. It is an ideative.

THE PROGRESSION OF THE ANCIENT CHARACTER TO PRESENT CHARACTER | PRONUNCIATION

戋 戋 走 走 武	wǔ

161

ANCIENT CHARACTER	PRESENT FORM	SIMPLIFIED FORM	PRESENT MEANING
罗	見	见	see, catch sight of

' 罗 ' combines ' ⌒ eye', and ' ₹ person'.
A person sitting on the floor with eyes wide open. He must
have seen something! The word is an ideative.

THE PROGRESSION OF THE ANCIENT CHARACTER TO PRESENT CHARACTER

罗 罗 罗 見 見 見

PRONUNCIATION

jiàn

ANCIENT CHARACTER	PRESENT FORM	SIMPLIFIED FORM	PRESENT MEANING
眷	看	看	see, look at, watch

'眷' combines '⺕ hand', and ' 目 eye'.
Put a hand over one's eyes in order to see clearly.
The word is an ideative.

THE PROGRESSION OF THE ANCIENT CHARACTER TO PRESENT CHARACTER	PRONUNCIATION
眷 看	kàn

ANCIENT CHARACTER	PRESENT FORM	SIMPLIFIED FORM	PRESENT MEANING
覓	覓	觅	look for, hunt for, seek

 — hand
— eye

One uses one's hands and eyes to look for lost items.

THE PROGRESSION OF THE ANCIENT CHARACTER TO PRESENT CHARACTER	PRONUNCIATION
覓 覓 覓	mì

164

ANCIENT CHARACTER	PRESENT FORM	SIMPLIFIED FORM	PRESENT MEANING
冒	冒	冒	emit, send out, give off, take the risk of

— hat

— eye

'冒' was the original word for hat. Hat is on one's head over the eye. If one's eyes are covered by a hat when one proceeds, one has to take some risk. It implies 'risks'. It is an ideative.

Hat is then written as '帽'.

THE PROGRESSION OF THE ANCIENT CHARACTER TO PRESENT CHARACTER   **PRONUNCIATION**

	PRONUNCIATION
冒 冒 冒	mào

ANCIENT CHARACTER	PRESENT FORM	SIMPLIFIED FORM	PRESENT MEANING
睡	睡	睡	sleep

'睡' combines ' 目 eye', and ' 垂 hanging down'.
When one's eye lids hang down, he is most likely sleeping.
'睡' takes the sound of ' 垂 '.

THE PROGRESSION OF THE ANCIENT CHARACTER TO PRESENT CHARACTER	PRONUNCIATION
睡 睡	shuì

166

ANCIENT CHARACTER	PRESENT FORM	SIMPLIFIED FORM	PRESENT MEANING
名	名	名	name, title

moon ————— 名
mouth —————

In the dark of night, people need to call out their names in order to be identified. The word is an ideative.

THE PROGRESSION OF THE ANCIENT CHARACTER TO PRESENT CHARACTER	PRONUNCIATION
叩 卮 名 名	míng

中國文字

167

ANCIENT CHARACTER	PRESENT FORM	SIMPLIFIED FORM	PRESENT MEANING
兄	兄	兄	elder brother, a courteous form of address between men.

— mouth
— person

'兄' looks like a person kneeling down, and emphasis is given to his mouth. It indicates that he has the authority to teach or give orders. Its original meaning was 'elder brother'. The word is an ideative.

THE PROGRESSION OF THE ANCIENT CHARACTER TO PRESENT CHARACTER

兄 兄 兄 兄	PRONUNCIATION
	xiōng

ANCIENT CHARACTER	PRESENT FORM	SIMPLIFIED FORM	PRESENT MEANING
䇂	言	言	speech, word, say, talk

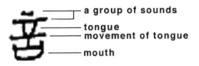

— a group of sounds
— tongue
— movement of tongue
— mouth

Sound comes from the movement of the tongue in the mouth. The '亠' indicates a group of sounds being sent out. The word is an indicative.

THE PROGRESSION OF THE ANCIENT CHARACTER TO PRESENT CHARACTER	PRONUNCIATION
䇂 䇂 音 䇂 言	yán

169

ANCIENT CHARACTER	PRESENT FORM	SIMPLIFIED FORM	PRESENT MEANING
𡆥	音	音	sound, music

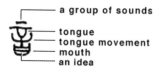

— a group of sounds
— tongue
— tongue movement
— mouth
— an idea

The word combines '𡆥 sound from mouth', and '— an idea'.
A group of sounds from one's mouth to express one's own idea or thought.

THE PROGRESSION OF THE ANCIENT CHARACTER TO PRESENT CHARACTER   PRONUNCIATION

𡆥 𡆥 𡆥 音 音	yīn

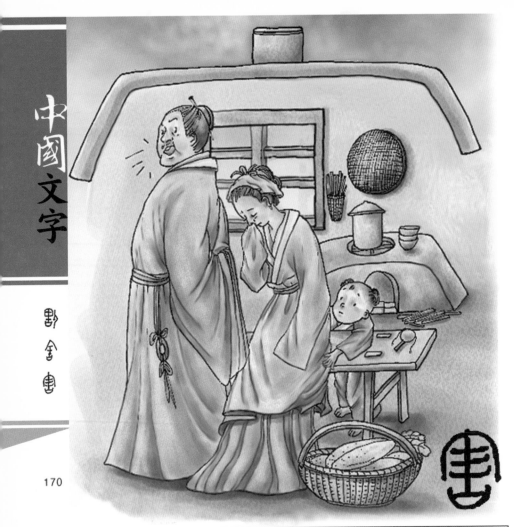

ANCIENT CHARACTER	PRESENT FORM	SIMPLIFIED FORM	PRESENT MEANING
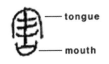	害	害	evil, harm, calamity

— tongue

— mouth

'害' combines '舌 tongue' and '口 mouth'. Hurt and damage always come from words of people's mouths. Its original meaning was 'harm'. The word is an ideative.

THE PROGRESSION OF THE ANCIENT CHARACTER TO PRESENT CHARACTER | **PRONUNCIATION**

害 金 害 害 | hài

ANCIENT CHARACTER	PRESENT FORM	SIMPLIFIED FORM	PRESENT MEANING
喜	喜	喜	happy, delighted, a happy event/occasion for celebration

'喜' combines '壴 drum', and ' ㅂ mouth'.
One plays drum and sings, he or she shall be very happy,
or there should be reason to celebrate. Its original meaning
was 'happy', and 'a happy event'.
The word is an ideative.

THE PROGRESSION OF THE ANCIENT CHARACTER TO PRESENT CHARACTER | PRONUNCIATION

喜 喜 喜 喜 喜	xǐ

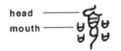

中國文字

172

ANCIENT CHARACTER	PRESENT FORM	SIMPLIFIED FORM	PRESENT MEANING
			clamor, hubbub, arrogant

head ——
mouth ——

A lot of people are speaking, the person in the midst of them seems to be annoyed by the noise. Its original meaning was 'noisy'.

THE PROGRESSION OF THE ANCIENT CHARACTER TO PRESENT CHARACTER　　PRONUNCIATION

| | xiāo |

173

ANCIENT CHARACTER	PRESENT FORM	SIMPLIFIED FORM	PRESENT MEANING
哭	哭	哭	cry, weep, sob, wail

eye ———
water ———
— mouth
— dog

'⊕川' is water from the eye. That is tears from eyes when one cries. '哭' is a dog wailing out loudly. The sound is as sad as one cries. Its original meaning was 'cry'.

THE PROGRESSION OF THE ANCIENT CHARACTER TO PRESENT CHARACTER   PRONUNCIATION

				kū

174

ANCIENT CHARACTER	PRESENT FORM	SIMPLIFIED FORM	PRESENT MEANING
𦣻	息	息	breath, rest

 — nose
— heart

The ancient Chinese thought that air entered through the nose and reached the heart. The original meaning of the word was the air that moved in and out through the nose.

THE PROGRESSION OF THE ANCIENT CHARACTER TO PRESENT CHARACTER | PRONUNCIATION

| 𦣻 𦣻 𦣻 息 | xī |

ANCIENT CHARACTER	PRESENT FORM	SIMPLIFIED FORM	PRESENT MEANING
獉	嗅	嗅	smell, scent, sniff

— nose
— dog

'獉' combines ' 自 nose', and ' 犬 dog'. Since a dog's sense of smell is very strong, it always uses the sense in identification of different objects. Its original meaning was 'the action of smelling' and also 'odor' The word is an ideative.

THE PROGRESSION OF THE ANCIENT CHARACTER TO PRESENT CHARACTER | PRONUNCIATION

獉 獉 臭 嗅	xiù

176

ANCIENT CHARACTER	PRESENT FORM	SIMPLIFIED FORM	PRESENT MEANING
自畀	自畀	自畀	nose

'自' is the original word for nose. It was used very often as 'me', therefore, a new word which served the meaning for 'nose' was formed.
'畀 connected upward' which pronounced similar to '自', was added below '自'. '鼻' becomes the upper passage which leads the air in and out.
'鼻' is a transmissive. *(p.319)*

Transmissive: The pronunciation of a word may have slight variation in differnt places and times. Therefore, a word with similar sound was added to the original word to reflect the change of pronunciation.

THE PROGRESSION OF THE ANCIENT CHARACTER TO PRESENT CHARACTER   **PRONUNCIATION**

自畀 自畀 鼻 鼻	bí

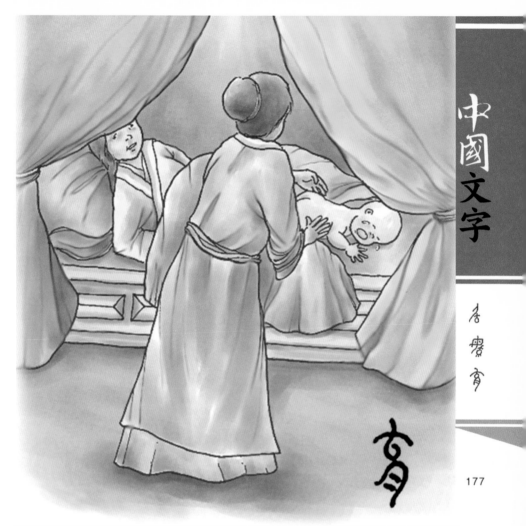

ANCIENT CHARACTER	PRESENT FORM	SIMPLIFIED FORM	PRESENT MEANING
育	育	育	give birth to, raise, bring up

' 古 ' is the word ' 子 child' written upside down.
' 月 ' means muscle, or from the body.
When a baby is born, he or she will come out from it's mother's body head first which resembles the character ' 古 '.
The word is an ideative.

THE PROGRESSION OF THE ANCIENT CHARACTER TO PRESENT CHARACTER	PRONUNCIATION
育 育 育 育 育	yù

炙
炙

ANCIENT CHARACTER	PRESENT FORM	SIMPLIFIED FORM	PRESENT MEANING
炙	炙	炙	roast, hot

'炙' combines '月 meat', and '火 fire'.
A piece of meat is put on the fire, which will result in a piece of roasted meat. Its original meaning was 'roasted meat'.
The word is an ideative.

THE PROGRESSION OF THE ANCIENT CHARACTER TO PRESENT CHARACTER PRONUNCIATION

炙　炙	zhì

ANCIENT CHARACTER	PRESENT FORM	SIMPLIFIED FORM	PRESENT MEANING
肎	有	有	have, possess, there is

'肎' combines '⺈ hand', and '月 meat'.
A person holds a piece of meat in his hand suggesting that he owns that piece of meat. Meat was very expensive in ancient China. Its original meaning was 'have', or 'own'.
The word is an ideative.

THE PROGRESSION OF THE ANCIENT CHARACTER TO PRESENT CHARACTER

	PRONUNCIATION
⺈ 肞 肎 ⿰ 肎 有	yǒu

ANCIENT CHARACTER	PRESENT FORM	SIMPLIFIED FORM	PRESENT MEANING
祭	祭	祭	hold a memorial ceremony for, worship heaven

'祭' combines '月 meat', '又 hand', and '示 the supernatural force'. In ancient times, people presented meat in rituals in order to show respect to their ancestors or dead relatives. The word is an ideative.

THE PROGRESSION OF THE ANCIENT CHARACTER TO PRESENT CHARACTER	PRONUNCIATION
祭 祭 祭 祭 祭	jì

181

ANCIENT CHARACTER	PRESENT FORM	SIMPLIFIED FORM	PRESENT MEANING
取	取	取	take, get, fetch, adopt

— ear

— hand

'取' combines '耳 ear', and '又 hand'. Hunters would cut the left ears off of their prey to count how many they had got in a hunt, or show the ears around as trophies. Its original meaning was 'take'. It is an ideative.

THE PROGRESSION OF THE ANCIENT CHARACTER TO PRESENT CHARACTER	PRONUNCIATION
取 取 取 取	qǔ

蘑 馨 馨

182

ANCIENT CHARACTER	PRESENT FORM	SIMPLIFIED FORM	PRESENT MEANING
磬	聲	声	sound, voice

sound —— 磬 —— stick
ear —— —— hand
rock ——

A person holds a stick in his hand '戶' and hits it on the rock '石'. It makes a loud sound on the rock '声' and that is transmitted to his ear '口'. Its original meaning was 'sound'. It is an ideative.

THE PROGRESSION OF THE ANCIENT CHARACTER TO PRESENT CHARACTER   **PRONUNCIATION**

磬 馨 馨 聲	shēng

ANCIENT CHARACTER	PRESENT FORM	SIMPLIFIED FORM	PRESENT MEANING
聰	聰	聪	faculty of hearing, intelligent

'聰' combines ' 目 ear', ' 窗 window', and ' 心 heart'.
The heart opens up like a window to receive messages from the ear, which implies that the person should be able to observe the details of what he learns. Its original meaning was 'observation'.

THE PROGRESSION OF THE ANCIENT CHARACTER TO PRESENT CHARACTER | PRONUNCIATION

聰 聰 聰	
	cōng

中國文字

184

ANCIENT CHARACTER	PRESENT FORM	SIMPLIFIED FORM	PRESENT MEANING
𤯽	母	母	mother

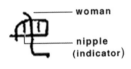

— woman

— nipple (indicator)

'𡤈' is woman, '𡤈' is woman with big breasts. Since women in the olden times needed to breast feed their babies, breast became a symbol for mother. The word is like a posture of a sitting mother breast feeding her baby. The word is an indicative.

THE PROGRESSION OF THE ANCIENT CHARACTER TO PRESENT CHARACTER

PRONUNCIATION

mǔ

ANCIENT CHARACTER	PRESENT FORM	SIMPLIFIED FORM	PRESENT MEANING
姓	姓	姓	surname, family name

姓 — woman — give birth to

'姓' signified women giving birth to children. Its original meaning was 'surname'. Since '姓' recorded the mother of the children, therefore, it is believed that children were named after their mother in ancient China. The word is an ideative and also a harmonic because '姓' takes the sound '生'.

THE PROGRESSION OF THE ANCIENT CHARACTER TO PRESENT CHARACTER	PRONUNCIATION
姓 姓 姓 姓	xìng

186

ANCIENT CHARACTER	PRESENT FORM	SIMPLIFIED FORM	PRESENT MEANING
安	安	安	peaceful, calm, quiet, safe

'安' combines ' 宀 house', and ' 女 female or daughter'. There is a daughter in the family. It implies that the house is serene and quiet. Its original meaning was 'serene and quiet'. The word is an ideative.

THE PROGRESSION OF THE ANCIENT CHARACTER TO PRESENT CHARACTER   **PRONUNCIATION**

安 安 安 安 安	ān

187

ANCIENT CHARACTER	PRESENT FORM	SIMPLIFIED FORM	PRESENT MEANING
好	好	好	good, fine, be fond of

好 combines '女 woman', and '子 child'.
A woman and her child are facing each other. In the mother's eye, her child is the best. In the child's eye, his mother is the best too. They are wonderful to each other. Its original meaning was 'wonderful'. The word is an ideative.

THE PROGRESSION OF THE ANCIENT CHARACTER TO PRESENT CHARACTER

PRONUNCIATION

好 好 好 好 好	hǎo

ANCIENT CHARACTER	PRESENT FORM	SIMPLIFIED FORM	PRESENT MEANING
	如	如	according to, as if, if

— mouth/saying
— woman

The ancient Chinese women needed to follow their fathers' teaching and husbands' advice. '如' looks like a woman listening to someone with authority. Its original meaning was 'follow', and 'listen to'. It is an ideative.

THE PROGRESSION OF THE ANCIENT CHARACTER TO PRESENT CHARACTER | **PRONUNCIATION**

rú

ANCIENT CHARACTER	PRESENT FORM	SIMPLIFIED FORM	PRESENT MEANING
婚	女昏	女昏	wed, get married

woman

evening

In olden times, marriage meant a woman returned to her husband's home. Women were considered to be 'yin' (recessive), so the marriage ceremony took place in the evening and they wore grey colored clothes. The word is an ideative and also a harmonic because '婚' takes the sound '昏'.

THE PROGRESSION OF THE ANCIENT CHARACTER TO PRESENT CHARACTER   **PRONUNCIATION**

婚 婚	hūn

中國文字

字宇字

ANCIENT CHARACTER	PRESENT FORM	SIMPLIFIED FORM	PRESENT MEANING
宅	字	字	word, character

 — house
— child

'宅' means a child is born in a house. Its original meaning was 'reproduction'. It is an ideative. Since a child will have many children when he grows up, that is like words which will increase more and more as time goes by. Later on, its meaning is changed to 'word'.

THE PROGRESSION OF THE ANCIENT CHARACTER TO PRESENT CHARACTER | **PRONUNCIATION**

字 宅 宅 字 字	zì

191

ANCIENT CHARACTER	PRESENT FORM	SIMPLIFIED FORM	PRESENT MEANING
孝	孝	孝	the love and respect for one's own parents

'夫' is the word 'old 夫' without the lower part. '子' means son.
The word '孝' looks like the son is taking care of his old parent.
'孝' also means that sons and daughters love their parents; they
will take good care of themselves because their bodies are the
presents of their parents, and convey their love to the next
generation as their parents do to them.

THE PROGRESSION OF THE ANCIENT CHARACTER TO PRESENT CHARACTER   PRONUNCIATION

孝 孝 孝 孝 孝	xiào

苷 苜 春

ANCIENT CHARACTER	PRESENT FORM	SIMPLIFIED FORM	PRESENT MEANING
萅 萅	春	春	spring, vitality

'萅' combines '艸 glass or plant', ' θ the sun', and '𦥑 two hands'.
Two hands are holding or caressing flowers under the sun.
It shows that Spring is the season in which plants grow abundantly.
Its original meaning was 'spring'. The word is an ideative.

THE PROGRESSION OF THE ANCIENT CHARACTER TO PRESENT CHARACTER **PRONUNCIATION**

萅 萅 春 春	chūn

ANCIENT CHARACTER	PRESENT FORM	SIMPLIFIED FORM	PRESENT MEANING
	旦	旦	dawn, daybreak

''combines '  the sun', and '— the horizon'.
The sun is rising over the horizon. It is dawn.
It is a beautiful picture of daybreak.
The word is an ideative.

THE PROGRESSION OF THE ANCIENT CHARACTER TO PRESENT CHARACTER	PRONUNCIATION
	dàn

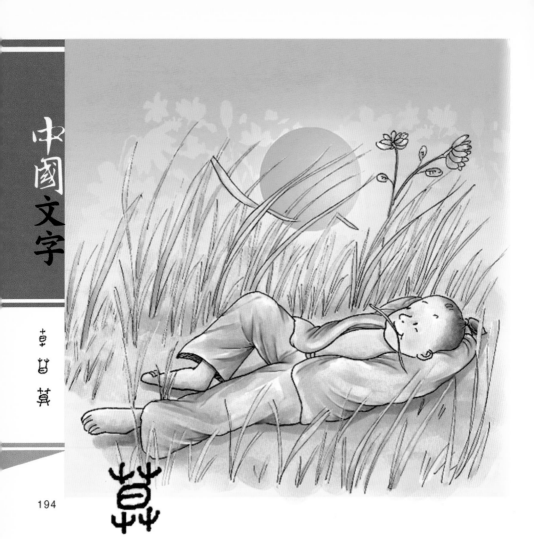

194

ANCIENT CHARACTER	PRESENT FORM	SIMPLIFIED FORM	PRESENT MEANING
茣	莫	莫	no, not, don't

'茣' combines '艸 grass or plant', and '日 the sun'.
The sun sets among grass and plants. It indicates the period of early
evening. It is an ideative. However, it was used very often as 'no longer
there' since the sun would disappear in the evening. '莫' then came to
mean 'not' and 'no'.
A new word for 'early evening' was made by adding the sun under '莫' to
indicate that the sun was still there -- 暮 .

THE PROGRESSION OF THE ANCIENT CHARACTER TO PRESENT CHARACTER   PRONUNCIATION

茻 茻 茣 茻 茻 莫 莫	mò

195

ANCIENT CHARACTER	PRESENT FORM	SIMPLIFIED FORM	PRESENT MEANING
			dusk, dark, dim

— low
— sun

' ' combines ' ' which is the short form of ' ' that means 'low', and ' the sun'.
When the sun sets, It is getting dark.
Its original meaning was 'sunset'.

THE PROGRESSION OF THE ANCIENT CHARACTER TO PRESENT CHARACTER	PRONUNCIATION
	hūn

中國文字

196

ANCIENT CHARACTER	PRESENT FORM	SIMPLIFIED FORM	PRESENT MEANING
暴	暴	暴	expose to the sun, sudden and violent (riot, flood), cruel, short-tempered

'暴 'combines' ☉ the sun', ' 㞢 comes out', '𦥑 two hands', and
' 米 rice grains'. A person takes out the rice grains with his hands,
exposes and dries them under the sun. Its original meaning was
'expose to the sun'. The word is an ideative.

THE PROGRESSION OF THE ANCIENT CHARACTER TO PRESENT CHARACTER | PRONUNCIATION

暴 暴 暴	pù

ﾌ ﾂ ﾌ

197

ANCIENT CHARACTER	PRESENT FORM	SIMPLIFIED FORM	PRESENT MEANING
ﾌ	夕	夕	sunset, evening

' 夕 ' looks like a half moon in the sky. The dash in the moon shows the reflection on it. Only half of the moon can be seen, it should be dim outside -- it is the period after sunset and the moon begins to rise.

THE PROGRESSION OF THE ANCIENT CHARACTER TO PRESENT CHARACTER	PRONUNCIATION
ﾂ ﾌ ﾌ ﾌ ﾌ 夕	xī

中國文字

198

ANCIENT CHARACTER	PRESENT FORM	SIMPLIFIED FORM	PRESENT MEANING
多	多	多	many, much, more, more than required

'夕' means a half moon - an evening. '多' means one evening after another. It suggests many evenings. By extension, it means 'many' or 'much'. The word is an ideative.

THE PROGRESSION OF THE ANCIENT CHARACTER TO PRESENT CHARACTER | PRONUNCIATION

多 多 多 多 多 | duō

199

ANCIENT CHARACTER	PRESENT FORM	SIMPLIFIED FORM	PRESENT MEANING
明	明	明	bright, brilliant, light

window
moon

sun
moon

It is the scene of moonlight coming through the window.
Or the moon and the sun are two illuminated objects in the sky that light up our world. Its original meaning was 'brightness'. It is an ideative.

THE PROGRESSION OF THE ANCIENT CHARACTER TO PRESENT CHARACTER

	PRONUNCIATION
明	míng

200

ANCIENT CHARACTER	PRESENT FORM	SIMPLIFIED FORM	PRESENT MEANING
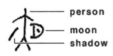	夜	夜	night, evening

'夜' looks like a person standing in the place where the moon is on his far right hand side while his own shadow is on his left. It indicates the night time. The word is an ideative.

— person
— moon
— shadow

THE PROGRESSION OF THE ANCIENT CHARACTER TO PRESENT CHARACTER | PRONUNCIATION

夜 | yè

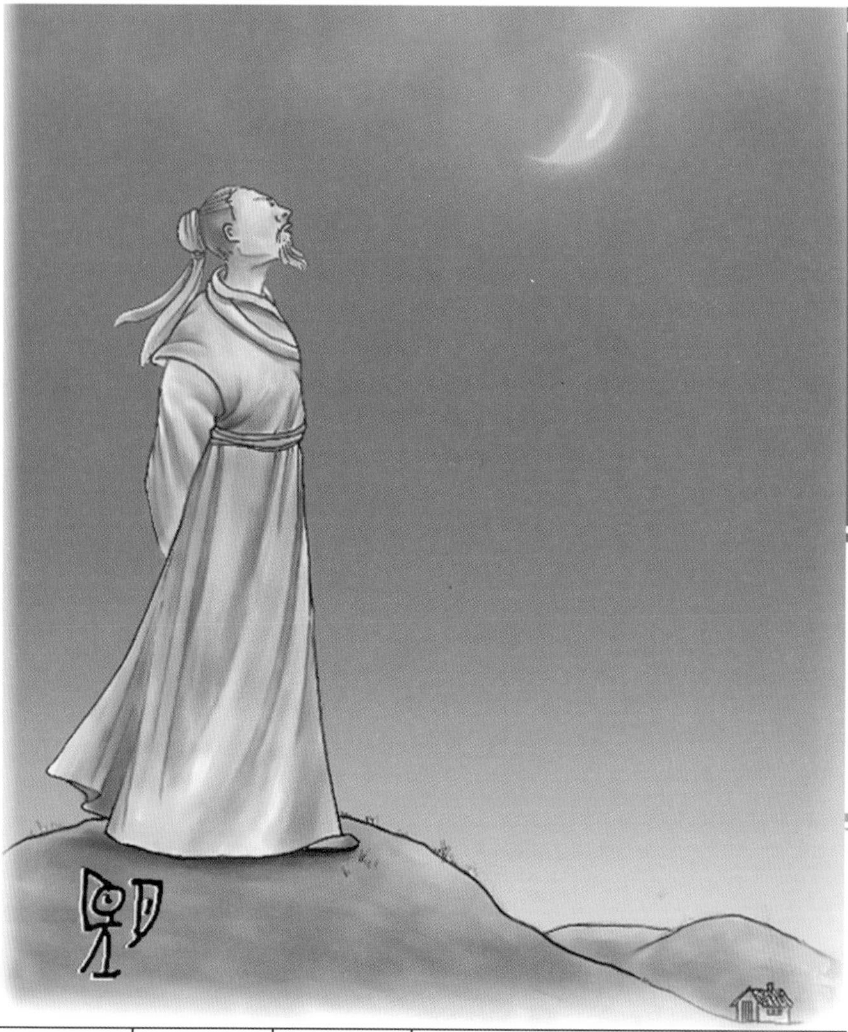

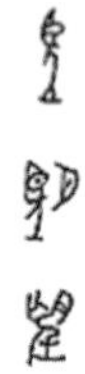

ANCIENT CHARACTER	PRESENT FORM	SIMPLIFIED FORM	PRESENT MEANING
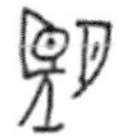	望	望	gaze into the distance, look over, look far ahead, to expect

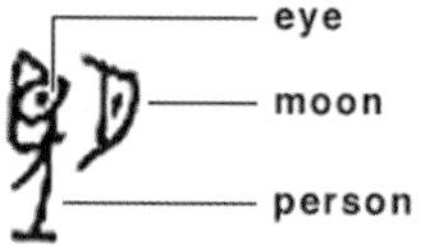

'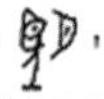' combines ' a person with his eye wide open', and ' the moon'.
A person stands on the ground looking up and staring into the distance. Its original meaning was 'gaze'.

THE PROGRESSION OF THE ANCIENT CHARACTER TO PRESENT CHARACTER	PRONUNCIATION
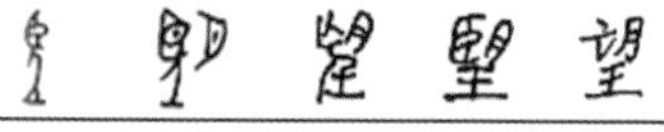	wàng

ㅏ
ᄯ
外

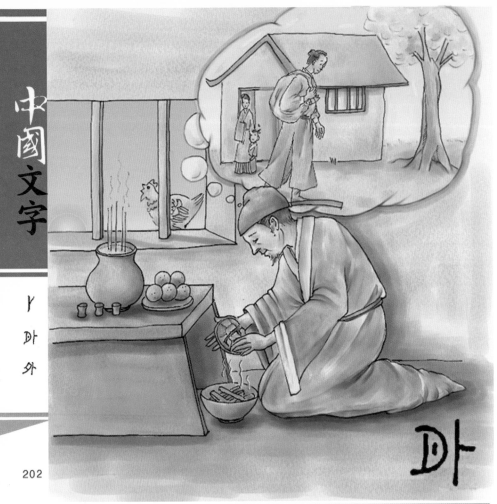

ANCIENT CHARACTER	PRESENT FORM	SIMPLIFIED FORM	PRESENT MEANING
ᄯ 外	外	外	outer, outward, outside

'外' combines ' ᄝ evening', and ' ㅏ the ritual' (the ritual in which a decision was made according to the cracks on a tortoise's back after smoking it for a time). In ancient times, ' ㅏ ' were performed early in the morning when a particular matter needed to be decided for that day. If ' ㅏ ' took place the evening before (ᄯ), there would be too much of a time difference and its accuracy would be reduced. Its original meaning was 'too far away'. It is an ideative.

THE PROGRESSION OF THE ANCIENT CHARACTER TO PRESENT CHARACTER **PRONUNCIATION**

Y ᄯ 外 外 外 外 外 外	wài

'雵' combines '𦥑 a person points to his eye', '⊘ eye', and '爿 bed'. A person sleeps on a bed with his fingers pointed towards his eye suggesting that he is seeing something in his sleep. He is dreaming.

203

ANCIENT CHARACTER	PRESENT FORM	SIMPLIFIED FORM	PRESENT MEANING
雵 夢	夢	梦	dream

— eye lashes
— eye
— night

A person sleeps at night, his eyes and eye lashes keep moving. It suggests that he is having a dream. The word is an ideative.

THE PROGRESSION OF THE ANCIENT CHARACTER TO PRESENT CHARACTER | PRONUNCIATION

| 雵 𦥆 䁦 夢 夢 | mèng |

204

ANCIENT CHARACTER	PRESENT FORM	SIMPLIFIED FORM	PRESENT MEANING
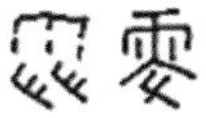 霏霎	雪	雪	snow

 — rain
— snowflakes —

The original meaning of the word was 'the frozen rain that carries snowflakes'.

THE PROGRESSION OF THE ANCIENT CHARACTER TO PRESENT CHARACTER | PRONUNCIATION

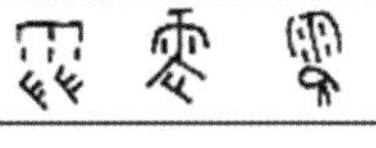

xuě

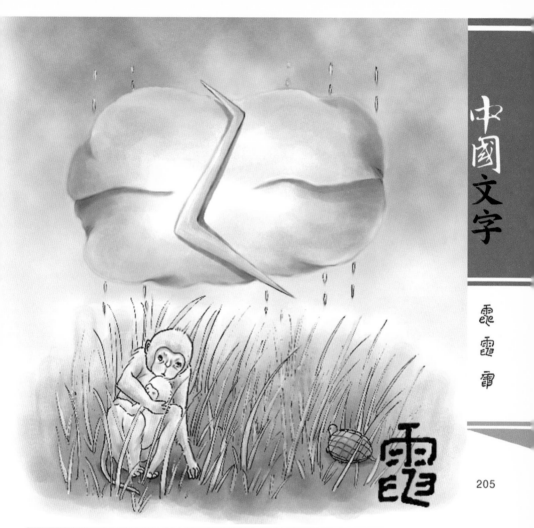

ANCIENT CHARACTER	PRESENT FORM	SIMPLIFIED FORM	PRESENT MEANING
電	電	电	electricity, lightning

— rain
— lightning
— collsion of clouds

It was believed that the cause of lightning was from the collision of the dominant and recessive forces from the clouds during a rain storm. The word explains the phenomenon of lightning. It is an ideative.

THE PROGRESSION OF THE ANCIENT CHARACTER TO PRESENT CHARACTER   PRONUNCIATION

霝 霝 電 電 電	diàn

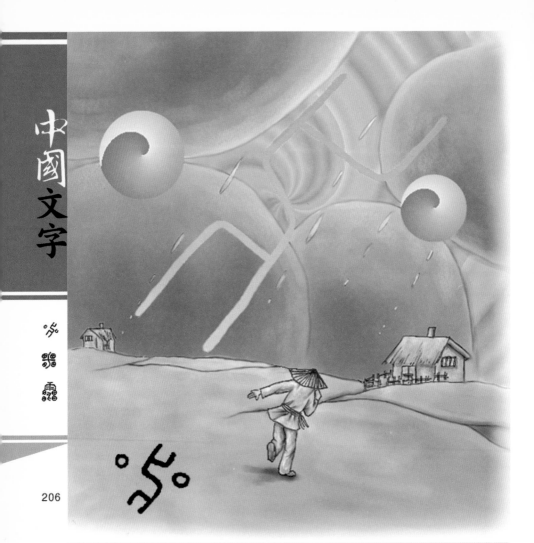

206

ANCIENT CHARACTER	PRESENT FORM	SIMPLIFIED FORM	PRESENT MEANING
	雷	雷	thunder

Thunder is a very loud sound that always goes with lightning and rainfall.

lightning
continuous thunder

rain
thunder
lightning

THE PROGRESSION OF THE ANCIENT CHARACTER TO PRESENT CHARACTER | PRONUNCIATION

	léi

災

災

207

ANCIENT CHARACTER	PRESENT FORM	SIMPLIFIED FORM	PRESENT MEANING
災	災	灾	calamity, disaster

'巛' means a great flow of water. '火' means fire.
A great flow of water and an uncontrollable fire can be a disaster.
Its original meaning was 'disaster'. The word is an ideative.

THE PROGRESSION OF THE ANCIENT CHARACTER TO PRESENT CHARACTER	PRONUNCIATION
災 災 災 災 災	zāi

ANCIENT CHARACTER	PRESENT FORM	SIMPLIFIED FORM	PRESENT MEANING
罙火	黑	黑	black, dark, secret, wicked

As the fire rises up '炎', the smoke finds its way through the window/chimney '田'. The smoke leaves a layer of residue on the wall of the window/chimney. The color is black.
The word is an ideative.

THE PROGRESSION OF THE ANCIENT CHARACTER TO PRESENT CHARACTER | PRONUNCIATION

罙 罙 炎 炎 黑	hēi

中國文字

ANCIENT CHARACTER	PRESENT FORM	SIMPLIFIED FORM	PRESENT MEANING
光	光	光	light, ray, brightness, luster, honor

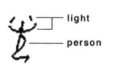

— light

— person

'光' looks like some light is shining over the head of a person who is kneeling down. If light is behind and over one's head, there will be brightness in front of that person. Its original meaning was 'brightness'. It is an ideative.

THE PROGRESSION OF THE ANCIENT CHARACTER TO PRESENT CHARACTER **PRONUNCIATION**

光 光 光 光 光	guāng

210

ANCIENT CHARACTER	PRESENT FORM	SIMPLIFIED FORM	PRESENT MEANING
示	示	示	show, notify, express, instruct

'二' means up, the above, '小' means three lights: the light from the sun, the stars and the moon. In ancient times, people studied astronomy to decide whether they could do or take care of certain matters. Words containing '示' relate to rituals or supernatural force. The word implies 'reveal'.

THE PROGRESSION OF THE ANCIENT CHARACTER TO PRESENT CHARACTER   **PRONUNCIATION**

爪 示 丁 丌 示 示 示	shì

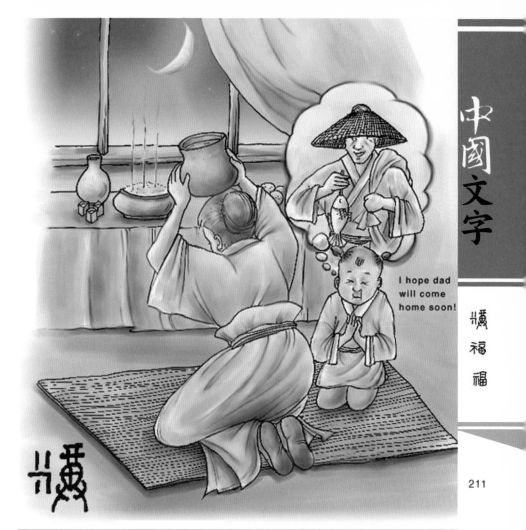

嘏
福
福

I hope dad will come home soon!

211

ANCIENT CHARACTER	PRESENT FORM	SIMPLIFIED FORM	PRESENT MEANING
	福	福	good fortune, blessing, happiness

— supernatural force
— wine container
— hand

One prays for blessings by consecration of wine to the supernatural force. Its original meaning was 'bless'. It is an ideative.

THE PROGRESSION OF THE ANCIENT CHARACTER TO PRESENT CHARACTER	PRONUNCIATION
嘏 福 福 福 福	fú

ANCIENT CHARACTER	PRESENT FORM	SIMPLIFIED FORM	PRESENT MEANING
㲱	沒	没	sink, submerge, disappear

'㲱' combines ' 水 water', ' ⦾ ripple', and ' 㐅 hand'.
Ripples are formed by dropping something into the water.
A hand goes down into the water, trying to get it out -- it probably
disappeared. Its original meaning was 'submerge'.

THE PROGRESSION OF THE ANCIENT CHARACTER TO PRESENT CHARACTER   **PRONUNCIATION**

㲱 沒 沒	mò

ANCIENT CHARACTER	PRESENT FORM	SIMPLIFIED FORM	PRESENT MEANING
活	活	活	live, alive

'活' combines ' 水 water', and ' 舌 tongue'.

Tongue needs water -- we have to drink water in order to stay alive.

THE PROGRESSION OF THE ANCIENT CHARACTER TO PRESENT CHARACTER | PRONUNCIATION

| 活　活 | huó |

中國文字

214

ANCIENT CHARACTER	PRESENT FORM	SIMPLIFIED FORM	PRESENT MEANING
	泰	泰	safe, peace

— a person
— two hands
— water

A person rescues another person in the water with his two hands. The rescued man is saved. Its original meaning was 'safe'. The word is an ideative.

THE PROGRESSION OF THE ANCIENT CHARACTER TO PRESENT CHARACTER — PRONUNCIATION

	PRONUNCIATION
泰	tài

中國文字

215

ANCIENT CHARACTER	PRESENT FORM	SIMPLIFIED FORM	PRESENT MEANING
㳄	永	永	forever, always

'㳄' looks like a swimmer who makes long waves and ripples in the sea. The original meaning of the word was 'long'.
Later on, the meaning of the word changed from describing the lengthy waves to the long duration of time. That is like a swimmer who feels he is always swimming in the middle of the sea but never reaching the shore.

THE PROGRESSION OF THE ANCIENT CHARACTER TO PRESENT CHARACTER   **PRONUNCIATION**

㳄 刋 㳄 㳄 永	yǒng

中國文字

216

ANCIENT CHARACTER	PRESENT FORM	SIMPLIFIED FORM	PRESENT MEANING
𡕄	冬	冬	winter

𡕄 —house
—sign of cold /cracks of ice

A house with piles of snow and cracks of ice in the front indicates that it is in a severe cold winter. Its original meaning was 'winter'. The word is an ideative.

—house
—droplet of water

Two drops of melting water dripping from the roof. This word suggests an earnest expectation for spring in winter.

—sun
—house

A warm house is as comfortable as under the sun -- a house is a haven from cold in winter.

THE PROGRESSION OF THE ANCIENT CHARACTER TO PRESENT CHARACTER **PRONUNCIATION**

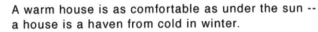

| | dōng |

ANCIENT CHARACTER	PRESENT FORM	SIMPLIFIED FORM	PRESENT MEANING
	寒	寒	cold

- house
- grass
- person
- shivering
- ice (sign of cold)

The word tells an experience of severe cold. A person is alone in his house: he covers himself with grass, his feet shiver because of the ruthless cold. The word is an ideative.

THE PROGRESSION OF THE ANCIENT CHARACTER TO PRESENT CHARACTER **PRONUNCIATION**

寒	hán

坐
出
坐

218

坐

ANCIENT CHARACTER	PRESENT FORM	SIMPLIFIED FORM	PRESENT MEANING
坐	坐	坐	sit, travel by

' ㅆ ' means two people facing each other, ' 土 ' means ground or soil.
Two people facing each other sit on the ground.
The word is an ideative.

THE PROGRESSION OF THE ANCIENT CHARACTER TO PRESENT CHARACTER   PRONUNCIATION

坐 坐 坐 坐 坐	zuò

219

ANCIENT CHARACTER	PRESENT FORM	SIMPLIFIED FORM	PRESENT MEANING
重	重	重	weight, heavy, serious, important

'重' combines '亻 person', '叀 heavy load', and '土 ground'.
A person carries a heavy load on the ground, he feels burdened!
Its original meaning was 'heavy'. It is an ideative.

THE PROGRESSION OF THE ANCIENT CHARACTER TO PRESENT CHARACTER | PRONUNCIATION

| 東 畐 蠢 重 重 重 | zhòng |

地
坤
土也

220

土也

ANCIENT CHARACTER	PRESENT FORM	SIMPLIFIED FORM	PRESENT MEANING
土也	地	地	soil, ground, land

Earth is compared to women who give birth. The word is an ideative.

土也 — soil
    female reproductive system

— uterine tube
— uterus
— vagina

THE PROGRESSION OF THE ANCIENT CHARACTER TO PRESENT CHARACTER | PRONUNCIATION

土也 坤 土也 地 | dì

221

ANCIENT CHARACTER	PRESENT FORM	SIMPLIFIED FORM	PRESENT MEANING
㯖	林	林	woods, grove

㯖 — tree

Two trees symbolize some trees.
There are some trees on a plain.
The word is an ideative.

THE PROGRESSION OF THE ANCIENT CHARACTER TO PRESENT CHARACTER | PRONUNCIATION

| 㯖 㯖 㯖 林 | lín |

中國文字

森 森 森

222

ANCIENT CHARACTER	PRESENT FORM	SIMPLIFIED FORM	PRESENT MEANING
森 森	森	森	full of trees, forest

 — tree

Three trees symbolize a lot of trees.
A lot of trees on a land implies a forest.
The word is an ideative.

THE PROGRESSION OF THE ANCIENT CHARACTER TO PRESENT CHARACTER	PRONUNCIATION
森 森 森	sēn

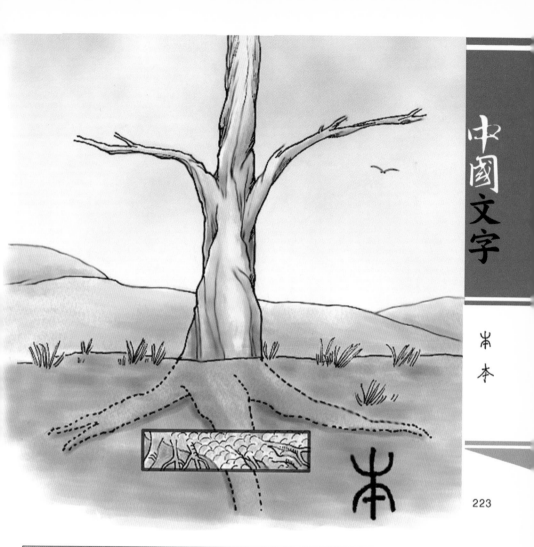

中國文字

木
本

223

ANCIENT CHARACTER	PRESENT FORM	SIMPLIFIED FORM	PRESENT MEANING
本	本	本	foundation, origin, capital

— tree
— the indication

The dash of the word indicates the lower part of a tree -- root. It implies its origin or source.
The word is an indicative.

THE PROGRESSION OF THE ANCIENT CHARACTER TO PRESENT CHARACTER

	PRONUNCIATION
本 本	běn

中國文字

224

ANCIENT CHARACTER	PRESENT FORM	SIMPLIFIED FORM	PRESENT MEANING
朱	末	末	tip, end, last stage

the indication

tree

The dash of the word indicates the upper part of a tree -- the offshoot. It implies the subdivisions of a main source, and also the last stage of a period or matter. It is an indicative.

THE PROGRESSION OF THE ANCIENT CHARACTER TO PRESENT CHARACTER

	PRONUNCIATION
朱 末 末 末	mò

ANCIENT CHARACTER	PRESENT FORM	SIMPLIFIED FORM	PRESENT MEANING
東	東	东	east

— tree
— sun

The sun rises behind the trees,
that direction is east.
The word is an ideative.

THE PROGRESSION OF THE ANCIENT CHARACTER TO PRESENT CHARACTER   PRONUNCIATION

東 東 東 東	dōng

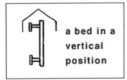

ANCIENT CHARACTER	PRESENT FORM	SIMPLIFIED FORM	PRESENT MEANING
爿	牀	床	bed

a bed in a vertical position

'牀' combines '广 house', and '爿 a bed in a vertical view, or the left half of a piece of wood (木)'.
A bed is a piece of wooden funiture in a house.

THE PROGRESSION OF THE ANCIENT CHARACTER TO PRESENT CHARACTER | PRONUNCIATION

爿 牀 牀 牀 床 | chuáng

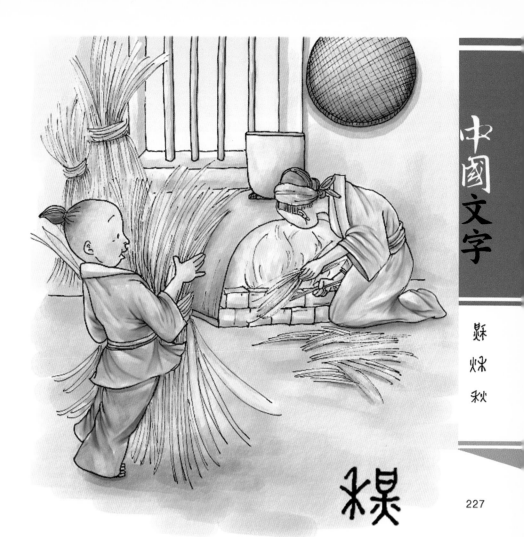

ANCIENT CHARACTER	PRESENT FORM	SIMPLIFIED FORM	PRESENT MEANING
穦	秋	秋	autumn

wheat and its dry leaves — pot — food — fire

Autumn is a happy season for farmers because wheat and other plants are ready to harvest. With hot food in the stove above the flaming fire, it is a time for enjoying the fruits of their hard work of the year.

THE PROGRESSION OF THE ANCIENT CHARACTER TO PRESENT CHARACTER	PRONUNCIATION
穦 縣 烌 秋 秋	qiū

ANCIENT CHARACTER	PRESENT FORM	SIMPLIFIED FORM	PRESENT MEANING
麥 麦	麥	麦	a general term for wheat, barley, etc.

麦
— spikes of edible grain
— toes and foot (dragging)

 pictures of feet with toes drawn upward

'麦' combines '耒 a kind of wheat' and '夂' is a posture of a person walking slowly, which symbolizes slowness. The wheat is planted in autumn and harvested the next summer. It grows slowly. The word is an ideative.

THE PROGRESSION OF THE ANCIENT CHARACTER TO PRESENT CHARACTER **PRONUNCIATION**

麥 来 麦 麦 麦 麥	mài

229

ANCIENT CHARACTER	PRESENT FORM	SIMPLIFIED FORM	PRESENT MEANING
香	香	香	fragrant, sweet-smelling, aromatic, scented

'香' combines '黍' corn', and ' 日 taste with mouth'.
The aroma of an ear of corn is fully savored when one is tasting it.
Its original meaning was 'aroma'.

THE PROGRESSION OF THE ANCIENT CHARACTER TO PRESENT CHARACTER	PRONUNCIATION
香 香 香	xiāng

中國文字

230

ANCIENT CHARACTER	PRESENT FORM	SIMPLIFIED FORM	PRESENT MEANING
罒貝	買	买	buy

— net
— seashell

Gathers seashells in order to buy -- seashells in a net represents having buying power.
The word is an ideative.

(net: fishermen used nets to gather or get fish, therefore, 'net' here means 'gather' or 'get'.)

THE PROGRESSION OF THE ANCIENT CHARACTER TO PRESENT CHARACTER   PRONUNCIATION

罒貝 貝 貝 買 買 買	mǎi

賣 賣 賣

231

ANCIENT CHARACTER	PRESENT FORM	SIMPLIFIED FORM	PRESENT MEANING
賣	賣	卖	sell

賣 —— out
—— net
—— seashell

Put out goods in order to get seashells.
Its original meaning was 'sell'.
It is an ideative.

THE PROGRESSION OF THE ANCIENT CHARACTER TO PRESENT CHARACTER	PRONUNCIATION
賣 賣 賣	mài

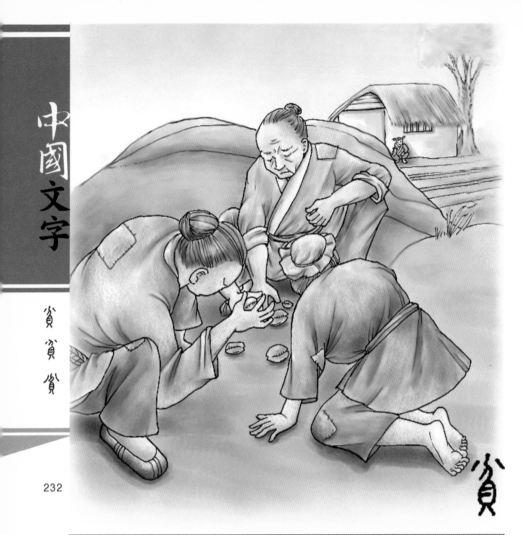

中國文字

232

ANCIENT CHARACTER	PRESENT FORM	SIMPLIFIED FORM	PRESENT MEANING
	貧	贫	poor, deficient

— share
— seashell

Seashells were the money currency at the time. If people have to share the seashells, the amount of the portions will become less. Its original meaning was 'a small share' which implied poor.

THE PROGRESSION OF THE ANCIENT CHARACTER TO PRESENT CHARACTER | PRONUNCIATION

pín

ANCIENT CHARACTER	PRESENT FORM	SIMPLIFIED FORM	PRESENT MEANING
𣪊 𣩍	敗	败	be defeated, lose

seashell
stick
hand

A person holds a stick ready to hit a seashell. He is going to destroy the valuable! It meant 'destroy' in the past. The word is an ideative.

THE PROGRESSION OF THE ANCIENT CHARACTER TO PRESENT CHARACTER | PRONUNCIATION

𣩍 𣪊 敗 败 | bài

ANCIENT CHARACTER	PRESENT FORM	SIMPLIFIED FORM	PRESENT MEANING
負	負	负	proud, carry on the back, to bear, to fail

person —
seashell —

A person carrying seashells around may be a rich man. The rich always count on money to fulfill their wishes. Therefore, its original meaning was 'count on'. The word is an ideative.

THE PROGRESSION OF THE ANCIENT CHARACTER TO PRESENT CHARACTER

PRONUNCIATION

| 負 負 負 負 | fù |

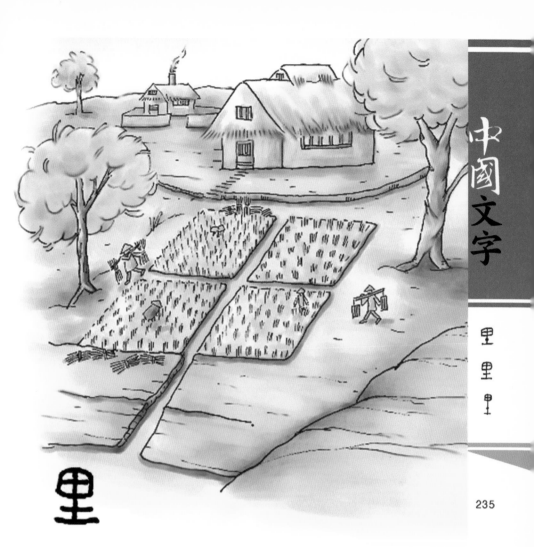

ANCIENT CHARACTER	PRESENT FORM	SIMPLIFIED FORM	PRESENT MEANING
里	里	里	residential area, neighborhood, inside, inner, lining

'里' combines '田 field' and '土 soil'.
Where there are fields and soil, there are people living.
The original meaning of the word was 'reside in'.
It is an ideative.

THE PROGRESSION OF THE ANCIENT CHARACTER TO PRESENT CHARACTER | PRONUNCIATION

| 里 里 里 里 | lǐ |

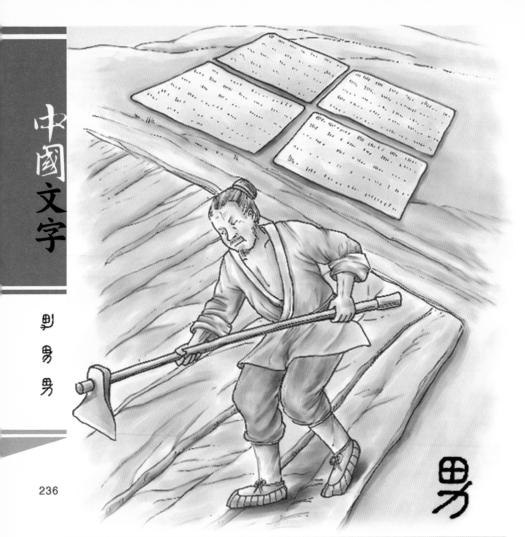

236

ANCIENT CHARACTER	PRESENT FORM	SIMPLIFIED FORM	PRESENT MEANING
男	男	男	man, male

'男' combines '田 field' and '力 labor or power'. In ancient times, men's work was to labor in the field. It meant 'male' in the past. The word is an ideative.

THE PROGRESSION OF THE ANCIENT CHARACTER TO PRESENT CHARACTER   **PRONUNCIATION**

男 男 男 男	nán

ANCIENT CHARACTER	PRESENT FORM	SIMPLIFIED FORM	PRESENT MEANING
𦰩	苗	苗	young plant, seedling

𦰩 combines 'ΨΨ grasses or leaves', and '⊕ field'.
The original meaning of the word was: the newly grown leaves
from crop seeds in a field.
The word is an ideative.

THE PROGRESSION OF THE ANCIENT CHARACTER TO PRESENT CHARACTER   PRONUNCIATION

苗 苗 苗	miáo

238

ANCIENT CHARACTER	PRESENT FORM	SIMPLIFIED FORM	PRESENT MEANING
	隻	只	one only, countable noun for most animals: cat, dog, bird, elephant...

—— bird
—— hand

'隻' is a bird in a hand.
Its original meaning was 'a bird'.

THE PROGRESSION OF THE ANCIENT CHARACTER TO PRESENT CHARACTER   **PRONUNCIATION**

隻 隻 隻	zhī

中國文字

雙
雙
雙

239

ANCIENT CHARACTER	PRESENT FORM	SIMPLIFIED FORM	PRESENT MEANING
雙	雙	双	even number(s), a pair of, two, twin, both

— bird
— hand

The original meaning of ' 雙 ' was 'two birds in one hand'.

THE PROGRESSION OF THE ANCIENT CHARACTER TO PRESENT CHARACTER	PRONUNCIATION
雙 雙 雙 雙	shuāng

中國文字

ANCIENT CHARACTER	PRESENT FORM	SIMPLIFIED FORM	PRESENT MEANING
雧	集	集	to get together, to gather, anthology, one volume of

雧 combines '雥 three or many birds', and ' 木 a tree'.
A flock of birds is in a tree. It implies 'flocks' or a gathering.
The word is an ideative.

THE PROGRESSION OF THE ANCIENT CHARACTER TO PRESENT CHARACTER | PRONUNCIATION

THE PROGRESSION OF THE ANCIENT CHARACTER TO PRESENT CHARACTER	PRONUNCIATION
雧 雧 雧 雧 集	jí

島
島

241

ANCIENT CHARACTER	PRESENT FORM	SIMPLIFIED FORM	PRESENT MEANING
島	島	島	island

—— bird

—— land

Island is a land surrounded by water and inhabited by wild birds.

THE PROGRESSION OF THE ANCIENT CHARACTER TO PRESENT CHARACTER | PRONUNCIATION

| 島 島 | dǎo |

242

ANCIENT CHARACTER	PRESENT FORM	SIMPLIFIED FORM	PRESENT MEANING
習	習	习	practice, review

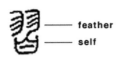
— feather
— self

'羽' is feather. It implies 'wings' here. '白' is a changed form for '自 self'. '習' is little birds practicing to fly with their wings. Its original meaning was 'practice'. The word is an ideative.

THE PROGRESSION OF THE ANCIENT CHARACTER TO PRESENT CHARACTER   PRONUNCIATION

| 習 習 習 | | xí |

243

ANCIENT CHARACTER	PRESENT FORM	SIMPLIFIED FORM	PRESENT MEANING
龖	龍	龙	dragon, imperial

'龍' is a worm with scales. It can be big or small. It can fly or swim. It combines three parts: the first is '辛', the shortcut of '童' from which '龍' takes its sound. The second is '月 meat or a creature', and the last is '巳' the shape of flying fins.
'龍' looks like a creature with fins dancing in the sky.

THE PROGRESSION OF THE ANCIENT CHARACTER TO PRESENT CHARACTER   PRONUNCIATION

	lóng

244

ANCIENT CHARACTER	PRESENT FORM	SIMPLIFIED FORM	PRESENT MEANING
血	血	血	blood

In olden times, people used animal blood in certain rituals for worship. The word looks like the blood is ready in the container. Its original meaning was 'blood'.

THE PROGRESSION OF THE ANCIENT CHARACTER TO PRESENT CHARACTER	PRONUNCIATION
血 血 血 血 血	xuè

ANCIENT CHARACTER	PRESENT FORM	SIMPLIFIED FORM	PRESENT MEANING
盜	盜	盗	steal, rob, thief, robber

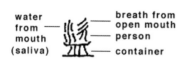

water from mouth (saliva) — breath from open mouth — person — container

A person with his mouth open and drools over the food container, there must be some delicious food in it. He is going to steal it! The word shows the motive of stealing - greediness. Its original meaning was 'steal'. The word is an ideative.

THE PROGRESSION OF THE ANCIENT CHARACTER TO PRESENT CHARACTER

PRONUNCIATION

dào

中國文字

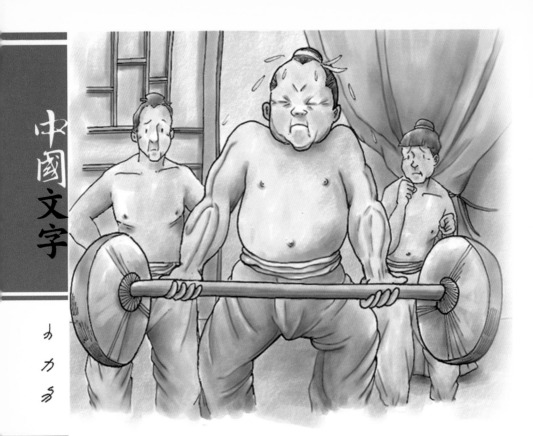

ANCIENT CHARACTER	PRESENT FORM	SIMPLIFIED FORM	PRESENT MEANING
㔹	力	力	power, strength, ability

'㔹' is like the shape of tendons found in the forearm when a person exerts froce to lift something very heavy. Its original meaning was 'tendon'. The word is a pictograph.

THE PROGRESSION OF THE ANCIENT CHARACTER TO PRESENT CHARACTER   PRONUNCIATION

㔹 㔹 㔹 力 㔹 屌 㔹 力	lì

ANCIENT CHARACTER	PRESENT FORM	SIMPLIFIED FORM	PRESENT MEANING
甬忠	甬カ	甬カ	brave, courageous

蕭 —weapon
—resort to

甬爪 The sound word ——— 甬忠
power or strength
heart ———
(thought)

There were different views and emphases in different times for the meaning of bravery.

THE PROGRESSION OF THE ANCIENT CHARACTER TO PRESENT CHARACTER

PRONUNCIATION

蕭 甬爪 甬忠 甬カ	yǒng

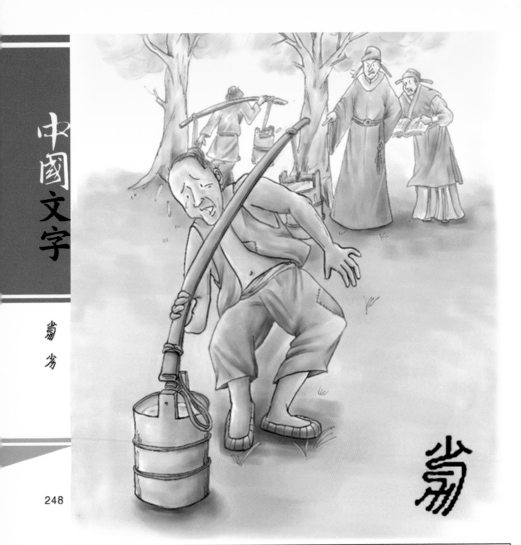

248

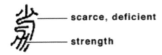

ANCIENT CHARACTER	PRESENT FORM	SIMPLIFIED FORM	PRESENT MEANING
劣	劣	劣	bad, inferior, of low quality

—— scarce, deficient

—— strength

A person who lacked strength or energy was considered to be weak in ancient China. Its original meaning was 'weak'.

THE PROGRESSION OF THE ANCIENT CHARACTER TO PRESENT CHARACTER | **PRONUNCIATION**

劣 劣	liè

ANCIENT CHARACTER	PRESENT FORM	SIMPLIFIED FORM	PRESENT MEANING
問	問	问	ask, enquire, inquire

 — door
— mouth

A person who wants to enquire
is at the door. Its original meaning
was 'ask'.
The word is an ideative.

THE PROGRESSION OF THE ANCIENT CHARACTER TO PRESENT CHARACTER　**PRONUNCIATION**

問 問 問	wèn

悶悶

250

ANCIENT CHARACTER	PRESENT FORM	SIMPLIFIED FORM	PRESENT MEANING
悶	悶	闷	bored, in low sprits

悶 —door
—heart

A heart is locked inside. That person is bored.
'悶' takes the sound of '門', and ' 也 ' stands for the state of mood, therefore, the word is a harmonic.

THE PROGRESSION OF THE ANCIENT CHARACTER TO PRESENT CHARACTER | **PRONUNCIATION**

| 悶 悶 | mèn |

ANCIENT CHARACTER	PRESENT FORM	SIMPLIFIED FORM	PRESENT MEANING
閃	閃	闪	dodging, sparkling

— door
— person

Its original meaning was that someone flashed past the door and peeked in from the gap.

THE PROGRESSION OF THE ANCIENT CHARACTER TO PRESENT CHARACTER　　PRONUNCIATION

閃　閃	shǎn

閒

ANCIENT CHARACTER	PRESENT FORM	SIMPLIFIED FORM	PRESENT MEANING
閒	閒	闲	leisure, idle, unoccupied, quiet

'閒' combines two words,' 門 door' and '月 moon'.
The moon can be seen through the gap of a door. Its original meaning was 'gap'. Later, the wirting of '間' replaced that of '閒'.
'閒' then came to mean 'leisure': one has the leisure to lean against the door and admire the moon.

THE PROGRESSION OF THE ANCIENT CHARACTER TO PRESENT CHARACTER	PRONUNCIATION
閒 間 閒 閒	xián

寶
瑠
陶

253

ANCIENT CHARACTER	PRESENT FORM	SIMPLIFIED FORM	PRESENT MEANING
寶	寶	宝	treasure, precious

'寶' combine '宀 house', '亼 ceramic container', '王 jade', and '貝 special kind of shell that was used as money at the time'.
Treasures like jade, shells, and valuable containers should be kept safely at home. Its original meaning was 'treasure'.

THE PROGRESSION OF THE ANCIENT CHARACTER TO PRESENT CHARACTER **PRONUNCIATION**

寶 瑠 陶 寶 寶 寶 寶	bǎo

254

ANCIENT CHARACTER	PRESENT FORM	SIMPLIFIED FORM	PRESENT MEANING
家家	家	家	family, home, household

— house
— pig

It was very common for Chinese families to raise pigs at home in ancient times because pork was a favorite meat for them.
Its original meaning was 'home'.

THE PROGRESSION OF THE ANCIENT CHARACTER TO PRESENT CHARACTER	PRONUNCIATION
家 家 家 家 家	jiā

宓 宓 寇

ANCIENT CHARACTER	PRESENT FORM	SIMPLIFIED FORM	PRESENT MEANING
宓	寇	寇	bandit, robber, the invading enemy

house — head of a person — stick — hand

A robber enters a person's house, hits the person on the head with a stick in his hand. Its original meaning was 'robber' and 'violent'. The word is an ideative.

THE PROGRESSION OF THE ANCIENT CHARACTER TO PRESENT CHARACTER

PRONUNCIATION

宓 宓 寇 寇 寇

kòu

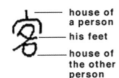

中國文字

256

ANCIENT CHARACTER	PRESENT FORM	SIMPLIFIED FORM	PRESENT MEANING
客	客	客	visitor, guest, caller

— house of a person
— his feet
— house of the other person

A person leaves his house, with his feet heading to another person's house. He must be a guest! The word is an ideative.

THE PROGRESSION OF THE ANCIENT CHARACTER TO PRESENT CHARACTER | PRONUNCIATION

| 客 舍 客 客 客 客 | kè |

室
金
室

257

ANCIENT CHARACTER	PRESENT FORM	SIMPLIFIED FORM	PRESENT MEANING
室	室	室	room

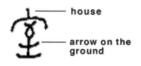

— house

— arrow on the ground

'至' is an arrow stuck on the ground which implies 'reach and halt', '宀' means a house. Its original meaning was 'a place in a house where people often stayed'. It might be a room for certain purpose, e.g. '臥室 bedroom', or '書室 library'.

THE PROGRESSION OF THE ANCIENT CHARACTER TO PRESENT CHARACTER   PRONUNCIATION

室 金 室 室 室   shì

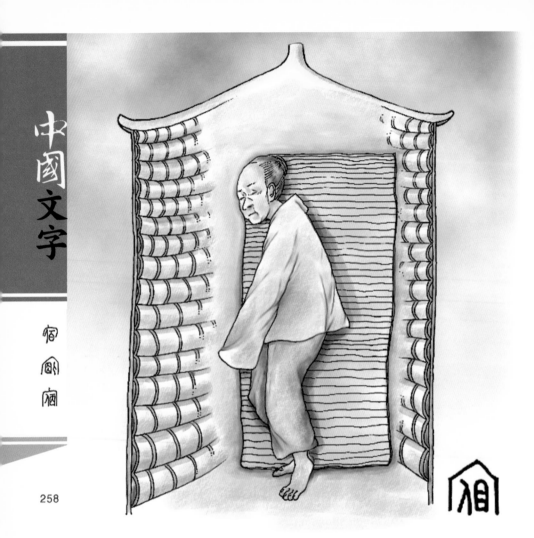

258

ANCIENT CHARACTER	PRESENT FORM	SIMPLIFIED FORM	PRESENT MEANING
㝛	宿	宿	lodge for the night, stay overnight

—— house
—— mat
—— person

A person sleeps on a mat in a house.
Its original meaning was 'lodge in'.
The word is an ideative.

THE PROGRESSION OF THE ANCIENT CHARACTER TO PRESENT CHARACTER | PRONUNCIATION

宿 㝛 㝛 㝛 宿	sù

剎
剎
剎

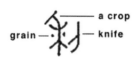

ANCIENT CHARACTER	PRESENT FORM	SIMPLIFIED FORM	PRESENT MEANING
剎	利	利	sharp, favorable, advantages, benefit, interest (money)

grain — 剎 — a crop / knife

To harvest a ripe rice crop with falling grains required a sharp knife. Its original meaning was 'the swift movement in harvest'. The word is an ideative.

THE PROGRESSION OF THE ANCIENT CHARACTER TO PRESENT CHARACTER   **PRONUNCIATION**

剎 剎 利 剎 剎 剎 利	lì

中國文字

260

ANCIENT CHARACTER	PRESENT FORM	SIMPLIFIED FORM	PRESENT MEANING
八刀	分	分	divide, separate, distribute, assign, allot

parts

knife

'八刀' is an object being divided by a knife. Its original meaning was 'separate'.

THE PROGRESSION OF THE ANCIENT CHARACTER TO PRESENT CHARACTER	PRONUNCIATION
八刀 八刀 分 分 分	fēn

ANCIENT CHARACTER	PRESENT FORM	SIMPLIFIED FORM	PRESENT MEANING
荪	芬	芬	sweet smell, fragrance

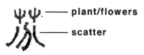

— plant/flowers

— scatter

The original meaning of ' 荪 ' was that the fragrance of flowers was scattered. '荪' is a harmonic, because it takes the sound of ' 分 ', and the fragrance is from ' 艹 plants'.

THE PROGRESSION OF THE ANCIENT CHARACTER TO PRESENT CHARACTER   **PRONUNCIATION**

荪 荪 荪 芬	fēn

ANCIENT CHARACTER	PRESENT FORM	SIMPLIFIED FORM	PRESENT MEANING
𢨋	初	初	at the beginning of, in the early part of, elementary

knife/scissors

clothes

The first step of making clothes is to cut a piece of cloth with a pair of scissors.
Its original meaning was 'at first'.
The word is an ideative.

THE PROGRESSION OF THE ANCIENT CHARACTER TO PRESENT CHARACTER	PRONUNCIATION
𢨋 初	chū

ANCIENT CHARACTER	PRESENT FORM	SIMPLIFIED FORM	PRESENT MEANING
𠬞	別	别	leave, different, distinction

'骨' is bone, '冎' is bone without meat attached to it. '刂' means knife. Using a knife to separate meat from the bone. The original meaning was 'disassemble'.

THE PROGRESSION OF THE ANCIENT CHARACTER TO PRESENT CHARACTER	PRONUNCIATION
𠬞 冎 別	bié

斑
斑
斑

264

斑

ANCIENT CHARACTER	PRESENT FORM	SIMPLIFIED FORM	PRESENT MEANING
斑	王廷	王廷	class, team

斑 — knife/chisel
— jade

Jade, which is a valuable jewel, is separated from stones by using a chisel. It implied to classify objects according to their qualities. It meant 'categorize' in the past. It is an ideative.

THE PROGRESSION OF THE ANCIENT CHARACTER TO PRESENT CHARACTER **PRONUNCIATION**

王廷 王廷 斑 斑 斑	bān

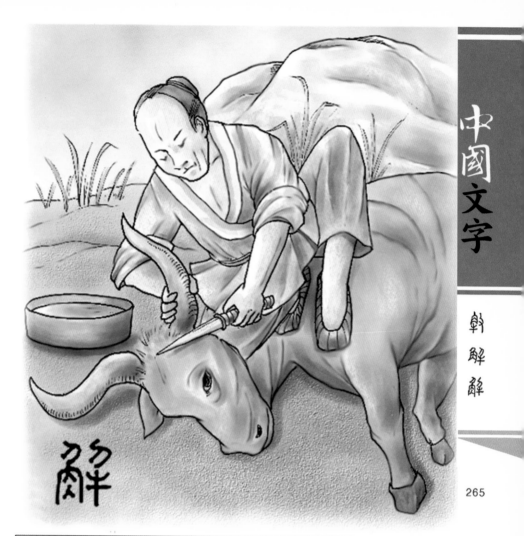

ANCIENT CHARACTER	PRESENT FORM	SIMPLIFIED FORM	PRESENT MEANING
觧	解	解	separate, divide, untie, undo, alleviate, solve

— knife
— cow
— horn

Use a knife to cut the horn out from a cow or to butcher a cow.
Its original meaning was 'disassemble'.
It is an ideative.

THE PROGRESSION OF THE ANCIENT CHARACTER TO PRESENT CHARACTER   PRONUNCIATION

斛　解　觧　解 | jiě

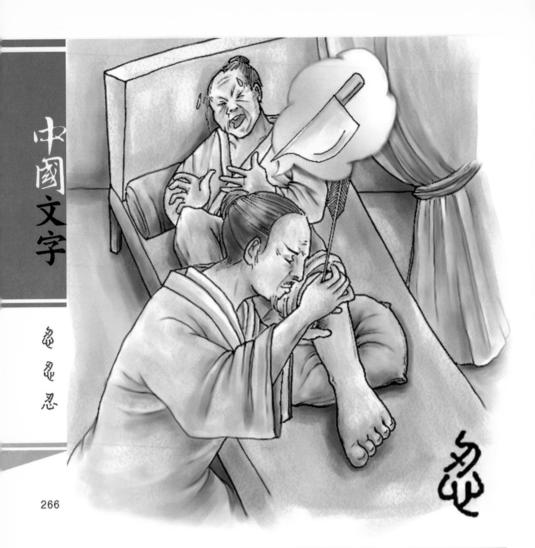

266

ANCIENT CHARACTER	PRESENT FORM	SIMPLIFIED FORM	PRESENT MEANING
	忍	忍	bear, endure, tolerate

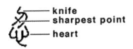
— knife
— sharpest point
— heart

One endures the pain that is as acute as the sharpest point of a knife thrusting into one's heart.
It is a harmonic: '刃' is the sound word, while '心' implies the endurance.

THE PROGRESSION OF THE ANCIENT CHARACTER TO PRESENT CHARACTER   PRONUNCIATION

	PRONUNCIATION
忍	rěn

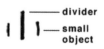

中國文字

267

ANCIENT CHARACTER	PRESENT FORM	SIMPLIFIED FORM	PRESENT MEANING
小	小	小	small, little, petty, minor, not important

—— divider
—— small object

The word combines ' ɪ ɪ small objects', and ' ʃ divider'.
Some small objects are being divided.
The word is an ideative.

THE PROGRESSION OF THE ANCIENT CHARACTER TO PRESENT CHARACTER   PRONUNCIATION

小 小 小 小 小 小	xiǎo

尖
尖

尖

ANCIENT CHARACTER	PRESENT FORM	SIMPLIFIED FORM	PRESENT MEANING
尖	尖	尖	top, tip, sharp, acute

尖 — small
　— big

If an object has its upper part small and lower part big, then it is sharp.

THE PROGRESSION OF THE ANCIENT CHARACTER TO PRESENT CHARACTER　　**PRONUNCIATION**

尖　尖	jiān

ANCIENT CHARACTER	PRESENT FORM	SIMPLIFIED FORM	PRESENT MEANING
少	少	少	few, less, deficient, not many, young

sand

A few grains of tiny sand.
Its original meaning was 'not many'.

THE PROGRESSION OF THE ANCIENT CHARACTER TO PRESENT CHARACTER	PRONUNCIATION
少 少 少 少 少	shǎo

ANCIENT CHARACTER	PRESENT FORM	SIMPLIFIED FORM	PRESENT MEANING
沙	沙	沙	sand, granulated, powdered, hoarse (sound)

water

a small amount of

When the water level is low (the amount of water is small), sand will emerge. It meant 'sand' in the past.
It is an ideative.

THE PROGRESSION OF THE ANCIENT CHARACTER TO PRESENT CHARACTER

PRONUNCIATION

沙 沙 沙 沙 沙

shā

ANCIENT CHARACTER	PRESENT FORM	SIMPLIFIED FORM	PRESENT MEANING
太	去	去	go, leave

太 —— person
U —— place

A person walks away from a place -- he is leaving. The word is an ideative.

THE PROGRESSION OF THE ANCIENT CHARACTER TO PRESENT CHARACTER	PRONUNCIATION
太 太 态 态 态 去	qù

中國文字

二 丄 上

272

ANCIENT CHARACTER	PRESENT FORM	SIMPLIFIED FORM	PRESENT MEANING
二 丄	上	上	high, higher grade, above, go up

—— an object

—— a base

The top dash indicates the upper position of an object. It is an indicative.

THE PROGRESSION OF THE ANCIENT CHARACTER TO PRESENT CHARACTER | PRONUNCIATION

| 二 二 上 丄 丄 上 | shàng |

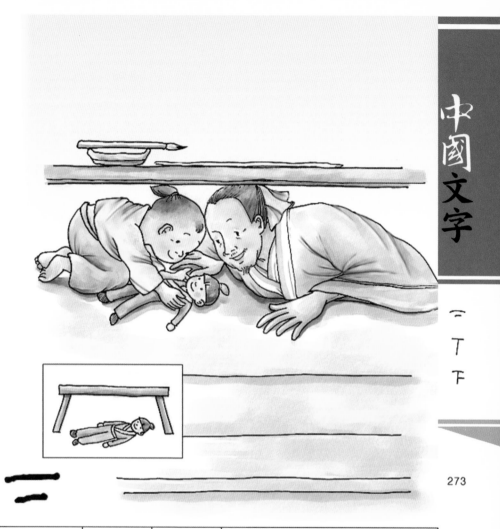

一 丁 丅

273

ANCIENT CHARACTER	PRESENT FORM	SIMPLIFIED FORM	PRESENT MEANING
二	下	下	below, down, under, underneath

 —— a base
—— an object

The indicator shows the lower position of an object.
The word is an indicative.

THE PROGRESSION OF THE ANCIENT CHARACTER TO PRESENT CHARACTER | PRONUNCIATION

二 二 下 丁 下 下 下 | xià

卡

274

ANCIENT CHARACTER	PRESENT FORM	SIMPLIFIED FORM	PRESENT MEANING
卡	卡	卡	wedge, get stuck, be jammed

卡 — up
— down

If something is stuck, it will neither go up nor down.

THE PROGRESSION OF THE ANCIENT CHARACTER TO PRESENT CHARACTER	PRONUNCIATION
卡	qiǎ

中
重
屮

275

ANCIENT CHARACTER	PRESENT FORM	SIMPLIFIED FORM	PRESENT MEANING
中	中	中	center, middle, in the process

中 combines ' ○ an object', ' | another object'.
Something went through, inside, or in the middle of an object.
It meant 'inside' in the past.

THE PROGRESSION OF THE ANCIENT CHARACTER TO PRESENT CHARACTER | PRONUNCIATION

| 中　中　重　屮　中 | zhōng |

狼趗後

後

ANCIENT CHARACTER	PRESENT FORM	SIMPLIFIED FORM	PRESENT MEANING
後	後	后	behind, back, rear

後

— small paces
— silk/linen material
— foot (dragging)

A person whose feet are tied up with rope is dragging behind in small paces. Its original meaning was 'late'. The word is an ideative.

THE PROGRESSION OF THE ANCIENT CHARACTER TO PRESENT CHARACTER	PRONUNCIATION
狼 趗 後 後	hòu

遙
道
道

ANCIENT CHARACTER	PRESENT FORM	SIMPLIFIED FORM	PRESENT MEANING
遙	道	道	road, path, way, doctrine, principle

main road
foot
trail

head
small steps
foot

'術' shows a foot (a person walking) on the main road. Main road implies the right way. Later, the foot was changed to a head, but the original meaning was the same.

THE PROGRESSION OF THE ANCIENT CHARACTER TO PRESENT CHARACTER | PRONUNCIATION

術 衛 遙 道 道	dào

中國文字

面
面

278

ANCIENT CHARACTER	PRESENT FORM	SIMPLIFIED FORM	PRESENT MEANING
面	面	面	face

contour of face
eye
nose

Since eye and nose are two outstanding features on the face, both the words 'face' from different times emphasize those features. It is an ideative.

THE PROGRESSION OF THE ANCIENT CHARACTER TO PRESENT CHARACTER

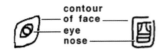

PRONUNCIATION

mìan

ANCIENT CHARACTER	PRESENT FORM	SIMPLIFIED FORM	PRESENT MEANING
士	士	士	scholar, person

The original meaning of ' 士 ' was 'male'.
The word looks like a man saluting.

THE PROGRESSION OF THE ANCIENT CHARACTER TO PRESENT CHARACTER	PRONUNCIATION
士 士 士 士	shì

中國文字

笑 笑

280

ANCIENT CHARACTER	PRESENT FORM	SIMPLIFIED FORM	PRESENT MEANING
笑	笑	笑	smile, laugh

wrinkles —
figure of a man with his head tilted to one side

'笑' combines '⺮ bamboo', and '夭' the sound word of '笑'. It is still a puzzle why bamboo links with laugh. However, '⺮' looks like the skin around one's eyes wrinkled when one laughs.

THE PROGRESSION OF THE ANCIENT CHARACTER TO PRESENT CHARACTER

PRONUNCIATION

笑 笑

xiào

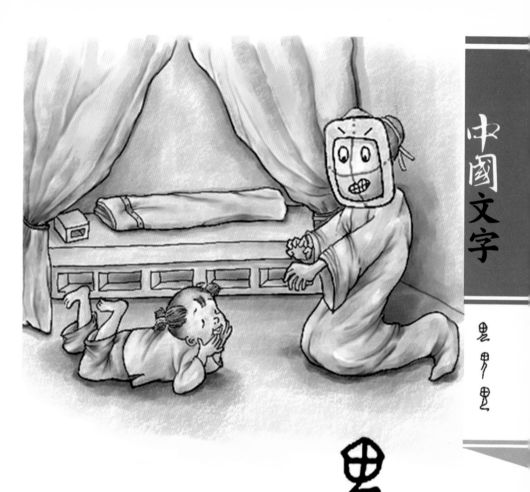

281

ANCIENT CHARACTER	PRESENT FORM	SIMPLIFIED FORM	PRESENT MEANING
畏	鬼	鬼	ghost, spirit

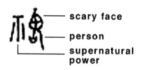
— scary face
— person
— supernatural power

'禐' combines '人 person', '由 scary face' and '示 supernatural force'. '禐' is originally from a human who has a scary face but possesses a supernatural power.

THE PROGRESSION OF THE ANCIENT CHARACTER TO PRESENT CHARACTER | PRONUNCIATION

畏 男 畏 禐 魄 鬼 鬼 鬼 鬼 | guǐ

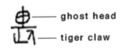

282

ANCIENT CHARACTER	PRESENT FORM	SIMPLIFIED FORM	PRESENT MEANING
畏	畏	畏	fear, fearsome

It is horrifying to see a creature with a ghost head ' ⊕ ' and a tiger claw ' 爪 '. The word is an ideative.

畏 — ghost head
— tiger claw

虎	鬼
tiger	ghost

THE PROGRESSION OF THE ANCIENT CHARACTER TO PRESENT CHARACTER | PRONUNCIATION

 畏

wèi

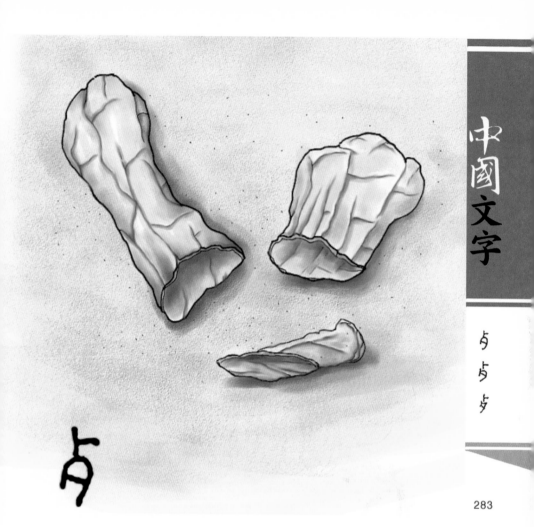

283

ANCIENT CHARACTER	PRESENT FORM	SIMPLIFIED FORM	PRESENT MEANING
歺	歺 歹	歹	bad, evil, vicious

cracks on the bone

The inside of the dried-up bone

'歺' looks like a piece of dried-up bone. Words combined with '歺' relate to death and also 'bad'. (death links with misery which is bad).

THE PROGRESSION OF THE ANCIENT CHARACTER TO PRESENT CHARACTER

PRONUNCIATION

歺 歺 歹

dǎi

夫者老

284

ANCIENT CHARACTER	PRESENT FORM	SIMPLIFIED FORM	PRESENT MEANING
夫	老	老	old, aged, old people, always

—— hair pin
—— person
—— walking stick

A person supporting himself with a walking stick indicates an old man. The word is an ideative.

THE PROGRESSION OF THE ANCIENT CHARACTER TO PRESENT CHARACTER   PRONUNCIATION

夫 耂 耂 老   lǎo

吊

285

ANCIENT CHARACTER	PRESENT FORM	SIMPLIFIED FORM	PRESENT MEANING
吊	弔	吊	hang, suspend, condole, mourn

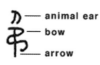

— animal ear
— bow
— arrow

In ancient times, people buried the dead by covering them with a thick layer of grass. People went to funerals, taking with them bows and arrows in order to scare away the animals that disturbed the dead. The word is an ideative.

THE PROGRESSION OF THE ANCIENT CHARACTER TO PRESENT CHARACTER **PRONUNCIATION**

弔 弔 弔 弔 弔 弔	diào

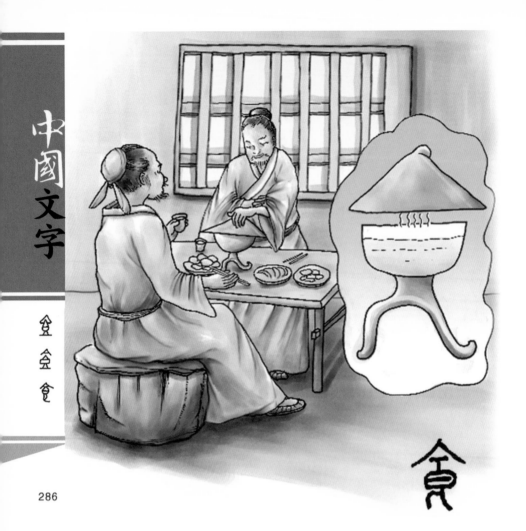

286

ANCIENT CHARACTER	PRESENT FORM	SIMPLIFIED FORM	PRESENT MEANING
食	食	食	eat

— cover
— food in container
— stand

There is some food in the container, implying there is food to eat. The word is an ideative.

THE PROGRESSION OF THE ANCIENT CHARACTER TO PRESENT CHARACTER | PRONUNCIATION

食食食食食食 | shí

287

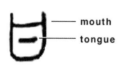

ANCIENT CHARACTER	PRESENT FORM	SIMPLIFIED FORM	PRESENT MEANING
甘	甘	甘	sweet, pleasant

— mouth
— tongue

' 甘 ' looks like a mouth with a dash in it. The dash indicates the position of the tongue which is the region most sensitive to delicious food. ' 甘 ' is a mild delicious sweet taste without spice. It is an idicative.

THE PROGRESSION OF THE ANCIENT CHARACTER TO PRESENT CHARACTER

甘 甘 甘 甘 甘 甘	PRONUNCIATION
	gān

288

ANCIENT CHARACTER	PRESENT FORM	SIMPLIFIED FORM	PRESENT MEANING
合	合	合	close, shut, join, combine, whole, agree

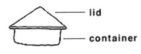

— lid

— container

'合' combines '⌒ lid', and ' 廿 container'.
Its original meaning was 'close'.
It is an ideative.

THE PROGRESSION OF THE ANCIENT CHARACTER TO PRESENT CHARACTER · PRONUNCIATION

合 合 合 合 合	hé

ANCIENT CHARACTER	PRESENT FORM	SIMPLIFIED FORM	PRESENT MEANING
			article, product

There are three articles being put together. Three symbolizes a lot of, therefore, it implies 'many kinds of articles' or 'articles in general'.

THE PROGRESSION OF THE ANCIENT CHARACTER TO PRESENT CHARACTER	PRONUNCIATION
	pǐn

ANCIENT CHARACTER	PRESENT FORM	SIMPLIFIED FORM	PRESENT MEANING
區	區	区	area, district, region

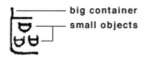

big container
small objects

Small objects are being put into a big container. Its original meaning was the area where things were being stored or gathered.

THE PROGRESSION OF THE ANCIENT CHARACTER TO PRESENT CHARACTER — PRONUNCIATION

qū

291

ANCIENT CHARACTER	PRESENT FORM	SIMPLIFIED FORM	PRESENT MEANING
匠	匠	匠	craftsman

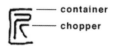
— container
— chopper

Chopper symbolizes the tools that carpenters use. This is a tool box of a carpenter. Its original meaning was 'carpenter'.

THE PROGRESSION OF THE ANCIENT CHARACTER TO PRESENT CHARACTER | PRONUNCIATION

匠 匠 匠	jiàng

中國文字

ANCIENT CHARACTER	PRESENT FORM	SIMPLIFIED FORM	PRESENT MEANING
向	向	向	direction, face to, turn towards

house ——
window ——

Windows were made facing to certain directions for ventilation and lighting in olden times. Therefore, the original meaning of '向' implied 'facing to' and 'direction'. It is an ideative.

THE PROGRESSION OF THE ANCIENT CHARACTER TO PRESENT CHARACTER	PRONUNCIATION
向 向 向	xiàng

魯
畜
高

293

ANCIENT CHARACTER	PRESENT FORM	SIMPLIFIED FORM	PRESENT MEANING
高	高	高	tall, high, of a high level or degree

— roof
— window of first floor
— door

'高' looks like a tall building with two floors. Its original meaning was 'tall' and 'high'.

THE PROGRESSION OF THE ANCIENT CHARACTER TO PRESENT CHARACTER PRONUNCIATION

魯 畜 冗 窩 高 高 高 高	gāo

中國文字

294

ANCIENT CHARACTER	PRESENT FORM	SIMPLIFIED FORM	PRESENT MEANING
	曰	曰	'曰' is the old word of 'speak', it is seldom used.

— words (indicator)
— mouth

— breath comes out when speaking
— mouth

The dash indicates a person's speaking. It meant 'speak' in ancient times.
'曰' is an indicative.

THE PROGRESSION OF THE ANCIENT CHARACTER TO PRESENT CHARACTER   PRONUNCIATION

曰 曰 曰 曰 曰	yuē

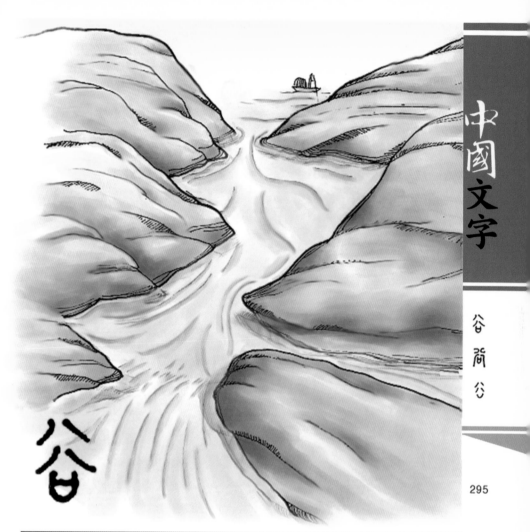

ANCIENT CHARACTER	PRESENT FORM	SIMPLIFIED FORM	PRESENT MEANING
谷	谷	谷	valley, gorge, cereal (an edible grain, as wheat or corn)

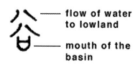

— flow of water to lowland

— mouth of the basin

Water is flowing from the mouth of the basin to the lowland. Its original meaning was 'valley'. The word is an ideative.

THE PROGRESSION OF THE ANCIENT CHARACTER TO PRESENT CHARACTER

PRONUNCIATION

谷 𧮫 公 谷 谷	gǔ

296

ANCIENT CHARACTER	PRESENT FORM	SIMPLIFIED FORM	PRESENT MEANING
曐 𣊫	星	星	star

The ancient Chinese thought that the stars had lives as they were
bright and many at one time, dim and fewer at other times. The Chinese
also would look up to the stars for consultations when they faced
dilemmas; the positions and degree of illumination carried specific
meaning to them. The word is an ideative.

THE PROGRESSION OF THE ANCIENT CHARACTER TO PRESENT CHARACTER	PRONUNCIATION
𣊫 𣊫 𣊫 曐 星 星	xīng

297

ANCIENT CHARACTER	PRESENT FORM	SIMPLIFIED FORM	PRESENT MEANING
			brilliant, glittering

 — glowing star

'⊙⊙' is a group of twinkling stars in the sky. Its original meaning was 'brightness'.
The word is an ideative.

THE PROGRESSION OF THE ANCIENT CHARACTER TO PRESENT CHARACTER | PRONUNCIATION

jīng

ANCIENT CHARACTER	PRESENT FORM	SIMPLIFIED FORM	PRESENT MEANING
南	南	南	South

plant
'屮' is the sound of the word

Plants in the south grow better than in other regions.

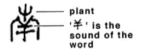

THE PROGRESSION OF THE ANCIENT CHARACTER TO PRESENT CHARACTER | PRONUNCIATION

nán

金 篆 鳳

299

ANCIENT CHARACTER	PRESENT FORM	SIMPLIFIED FORM	PRESENT MEANING
鳳	風	风	wind

'凡' means eight, wind blows from eight (different) directions.
'虫' means worm(s). '一' looks like the ground.
If there is wind blowing, there may be a change in air pressure and
worms underground will move or come out of the ground. So
whenever there is wind blowing, there are worms to be seen.

THE PROGRESSION OF THE ANCIENT CHARACTER TO PRESENT CHARACTER   PRONUNCIATION

月 金 鳳 鳳 鳳 風	fēng

中國文字

300

ANCIENT CHARACTER	PRESENT FORM	SIMPLIFIED FORM	PRESENT MEANING
	夏	夏	summer

sun ———

finger ———

person ———

'　' looks like a man pointing to the sun with his fingers. He wants to show how hot the sun is. The blazing sun indicates a summer.

THE PROGRESSION OF THE ANCIENT CHARACTER TO PRESENT CHARACTER   PRONUNCIATION

	xià

黄
黃
黃

ANCIENT CHARACTER	PRESENT FORM	SIMPLIFIED FORM	PRESENT MEANING
黄	黃	黄	yellow

The word is composed of two parts: '芄' means light,
'田' means the field.
The field under sunlight is yellow. To easily remember '黃',
you may call it Mr. Big Belly Huang, as the word looks like a
man with a big belly.

THE PROGRESSION OF THE ANCIENT CHARACTER TO PRESENT CHARACTER	PRONUNCIATION
東 灸 黃 黃 黃 黃 黃	huáng

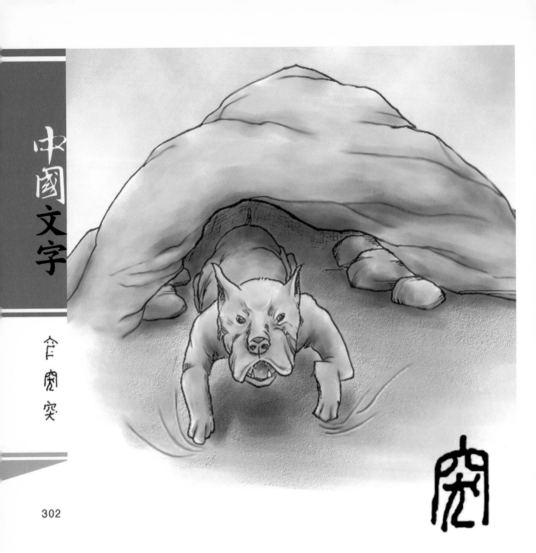

ANCIENT CHARACTER	PRESENT FORM	SIMPLIFIED FORM	PRESENT MEANING
𡧃	突	突	dash forward, sudden, projecting

— cave
— dog

A dog suddenly dashed out from a cave.
Its original meaning was 'sudden'.
The word is an ideative.

THE PROGRESSION OF THE ANCIENT CHARACTER TO PRESENT CHARACTER | PRONUNCIATION

倉𡧃突 | tū

半
坐
半

303

ANCIENT CHARACTER	PRESENT FORM	SIMPLIFIED FORM	PRESENT MEANING
半	半	半	half, semi

— eight

— cow

The shape of ' 八 eight' looks like separating an object into halves. The original meaning of ' 半 ' was to share a cow by dividing it into two halves.
The word is an ideative.

THE PROGRESSION OF THE ANCIENT CHARACTER TO PRESENT CHARACTER   PRONUNCIATION

半 坐 半 半 半 半	bàn

中國文字

304

ANCIENT CHARACTER	PRESENT FORM	SIMPLIFIED FORM	PRESENT MEANING
尺	尺	尺	ruler, a length unit (1 尺 =12 inches)

— knee cap
— indicator
— heel

In ancient times, the units of measurement were always taken from part of a man's body. The dot in the word indicates the length of one foot which is approximately the distance from the heel to somewhere below the knee cap. The word is an indicative.

THE PROGRESSION OF THE ANCIENT CHARACTER TO PRESENT CHARACTER

PRONUNCIATION

尺 尺 尺 尺	chǐ

ANCIENT CHARACTER	PRESENT FORM	SIMPLIFIED FORM	PRESENT MEANING
用	用	用	use, employ, apply

'用' combines '冊 middle, fit for', and '卜 a kind of ritual' *(p.202)*.
It meant that the consultation from the ritual was fit for applying into practice.
Another study said that it is a container that looks like a bucket. It is a pictograph of a bucket.
By extension, '用' meant 'use' or 'by means of' in the past.

THE PROGRESSION OF THE ANCIENT CHARACTER TO PRESENT CHARACTER | PRONUNCIATION

| 用 用 用 用 用 用 用 用 | yòng |

中國文字

金 釜
釜

金

ANCIENT CHARACTER	PRESENT FORM	SIMPLIFIED FORM	PRESENT MEANING
金	金	金	gold

金 — sound word
— soil
— gold

金 — sound word
— fire

'金' combines '土 soil', ' ' gold' and a sound word '亼'.
It was believed that gold was from soil. The two dashes are the formation of gold in soil.
'金', the earlier stage of gold, showing that gold was extracted by means of fire.

THE PROGRESSION OF THE ANCIENT CHARACTER TO PRESENT CHARACTER　　PRONUNCIATION

金 金 金 金 金 金 金	jīn

ANCIENT CHARACTER	PRESENT FORM	SIMPLIFIED FORM	PRESENT MEANING
𢦏	我	我	I, self, me

— weapon
— hand

'𢦏' was a lethal weapon used in wars with sharp teeth at one end.
Later, it was borrowed to mean 'I'.
'𢦏' then may be explained as: a person takes a weapon in order to defend himself.
the word is a borrowed.

THE PROGRESSION OF THE ANCIENT CHARACTER TO PRESENT CHARACTER   PRONUNCIATION

𢦏 午 我 我 我 我	wǒ

ANCIENT CHARACTER	PRESENT FORM	SIMPLIFIED FORM	PRESENT MEANING
發	發	发	send out, deliver, distribute, issue

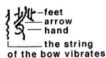 — feet
— arrow
— hand
— the string of the bow vibrates after the arrow is shot

 — feet
— arrow
— hand
— bow

With a hand holding an arrow on the bowstring, and two feet standing firmly on the ground, the arrow was ready to be shot.
The word is an ideative.

THE PROGRESSION OF THE ANCIENT CHARACTER TO PRESENT CHARACTER | PRONUNCIATION

發 | fā

Appendix

Topics of Interest

310

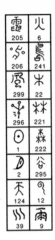

Seasons

Directions

312

Color

Measurements

Index / Alphabetical Order In Pronunciation

xīng	星 （星）	296
xíng	行 （行）	30
xìng	性 （性）	131
xìng	姓 （姓）	185
xiōng	兄 （兄）	167
xiū	休 （休）	110
xiù	嗅 （嗅）	175
xué	穴 （穴）	101
xuě	雪 （雪）	204
xuè	血 （血）	244

Y

yá	牙 （牙）	55
yán	言 （言）	168
yáng	羊 （羊）	66
yè	頁 （页）	54
yè	夜 （夜）	200
yī	衣 （衣）	100
yī	依 （依）	113
yīn	音 （音）	169
yǒng	永 （永）	215
yǒng	勇 （勇）	247
yòng	用 （用）	305
yǒu	酉 （酉）	84
yǒu	友 （友）	138
yǒu	有 （有）	179
yòu	又 （又）	42
yú	魚 （鱼）	72
yǔ	羽 （羽）	74
yǔ	雨 （雨）	9
yù	玉 （玉）	13
yù	育 （育）	177
yuē	曰 （曰）	294
yuè	月 （月）	2
yún	雲 （云）	12

Z

zāi	災 （灾）	207
zàng	葬 （葬）	123
zhǎo	爪 （爪）	76
zhēng	爭 （争）	141
zhèng	正 （正）	156
zhī	隻 （只）	238
zhǐ	止 （止）	49
zhì	志 （志）	135
zhì	至 （至）	96
zhì	炙 （炙）	178
zhōng	中 （中）	275
zhòng	眾 （众）	120
zhòng	重 （重）	219
zhōu	舟 （舟）	80
zhú	竹 （竹）	21
zhuō	捉 （捉）	145
zǐ	子 （子）	36
zì	自 （自）	47
zì	字 （字）	190
zǒu	走 （走）	159
zú	足 （足）	50
zuò	坐 （坐）	218

Supplementary Information

Six methods of making Chinese words

Pictographs
Words formed from objects that can be drawn.

e.g. ' 馬 horse', ' 鳥 bird', ' 人 people'.

They are pictures of the objects.

*There were 364 pictographs in Chinese characters, as recorded in A.D.121.

Indicatives
Indicators are added to words/signs for telling things that cannot be drawn, like directions, positions, numbers.

e.g. ' 寸 inch' — the dash indicates the distance from palm to the pulse.

' 本 base' — the dash indicates the root of a tree.

' 末 trifle' — the dash indicates the offshoot of a tree.

*There were 125 indicatives in Chinese characters, as recorded in A.D.121.

Ideatives
Words formed from words/signs which combine to suggest a new meaning.

e.g. ' 休 rest' — a man ' 亻 ' rests by leaning on a tree ' 木 '.

' 保 protect' — a man ' 亻 ' protects a child ' 子 ' by carrying him on his back.

' 林 a woods' — two trees ' 林 ' symbolize a woods.

*There were 1167 ideatives in Chinese characters, as recorded in A.D.121.

318

Harmonics
Words formed from two words/signs combine together; one stands for its meaning, and the other stands for its pronunciation.

e.g. ' 忍 patience' — ' 刃 ' is the sound word, ' 心 heart' implies persistence.

' 悶 bored' — ' 門 ' is the sound word. ' 心 heart' implies the feelings.

*Over 82% of Chinese characters are from harmonics, as recorded in A.D.121. Now it is estimated that over 90% of Chinese words are in this category.

Borroweds
Pronunciations always come first before the invention of words. Some existing words are then taken or borrowed to apply to some pronunciations; new words are formed with their own meanings by borrowing other words that have similar pronunciations.

e.g. ' 令 ' means 'give order'. Later, it is borrowed to use as 'your' and 'cause' because of their similarity in pronunciation.

Transmissives

The pronunciation of a word may have slight variation in different places (dialects) and times (the development of the language). Therefore, a word with similar sound is added to the original word to reflect the change of pronunciation.

Generally, the original word and its transmissive share three factors: they have the same meaning, similar pronunciation, and they are from one radical.*

e.g. ' 豕 ' means 'pig'. Later, ' 者 ' was added to indicate the change of pronunciation for 'pig'. Both ' 豕 ' and ' 豬 ' mean 'pig', have the same radical ' 豕 ', and have similar pronunciations.

' 自 ' means 'nose'. Later, one more word was made for 'nose': ' 畀 ' was added to indicate the change of pronunciation for 'nose'. Both ' 自 ' and ' 鼻 ' mean 'nose', have the same radical ' 自 ', and have similar pronunciation.

Footnote

*The numbers of pictographs, indicatives, ideatives and harmonics cited here were obtained from a book known as ' 说文解字 ' which explained Chinese words and their classifications. The book was written in A.D. 121.

319

*Radicals are root words which convey basic meaning. They may stand alone as most of the pictographs or combine with other words to become ideatives, harmonics, indicatives and transmissives. Besides, they can also tell the nature of the word, for example:

' 心 heart' — words combined with this radical relate to feelings, will power, passion or conscience.

' 日 sun' — words combined with this radical relate to sun, brightness, season or time.

References

Name of the book	Author	Publisher
常用漢字字源手冊 Handbook on Sources of Common Chinese Characters	王平、朱葆華 劉中富、吳建偉 臧克和 Wang Pin Zhu Baohua Liu Zhongfu Wu Jianwei Zang Kehe	南方日報出版社 Nanfang Daily Press
香港常用字字形精解 （1-2冊） The Analysis of commonly used Chinese Words in Hong Kong (1-2)	潘慧如 Pan Huiru	中華書局 Chung Hwa Book
圖說漢字密碼 （1-4冊） Decode Chinese Words (1-4)	唐漢 Tang Han	中華書局 Chung Hwa Book
認識國字部首 Introduction to Chinese Radicals	吳啟振 Wu Chichen	國語日報 Mandarin Daily News
文字的故事 Story of Chinese Characters	李梵 Li Fan	好讀出版 Howdo Book
有趣的部首 Interesting Radicals	布裕民 Pu Yumin	現代教育研究社 Modern Educational Research Society, Ltd
現代漢英詞典 A Modern Chinese-English Dictionary		外語教學與 研究出版社 Foreign Languages Teaching And Research Press

321

About This Book

Many of the words in this book were made more than three thousand years ago. They were found incised on the turtle shells and animal bones. They represent the oldest form of words discovered in China, known as 'jiaguwen', literally, 'shell bone writing'. Approximately 4,500 words of jiaguwen have been discovered, and about 2,000 of them have been deciphered. Jiaguwen includes not only pictographs but also five other classes of words (see p.318). The form of writing shows that, besides artistic skill, the ancient people had already developed a very mature and complex level of observation, reasoning, and comprehension.

The ancient Chinese recorded their lives in the form of words. Words tell their perceptions of this bewildering but wonderful world, their passions for the earth that nurtured them, their creation of a basic humanity, and their quests for their own identities – what they saw in themselves and what they pursued. You may find in this book some very uplifting words that bring out the best in a person, and may gain understanding of the framework of Chinese culture through them.

This book was orginally the teaching material I made for my daughter to learn Chinese. The first challenge I thought of was how to link a three thousand–year–old thoughts of people to a two–year–old child. To my amazement, I could easily see the bridge formed by their shared curiosity, naivety, and lively enjoyment of being on earth. I cannot forget the sight of my two–year–old toddling to me with her pigtails waving side–to–side for her 'little Chinese story'. I then decided to make the 'stories' worthy of her difficult trips.

The words are the sincerest way of the ancient people attempting to share their thoughts; certain principles and values in our lives are timeless, and so is the appreciation of the beauty of our earth. I hope readers can connect with the feelings in them, and enjoy the trip to the ancient past.

About The Author

Sukming Lo worked as a graphic designer for more than ten years. She has worked in a publishing firm, advertising firm, Crown Motor Ltd., and Hong Kong Government Post Office Department.

She had one year of unforgetable experience in teaching art in a high school on a small outlying island in Hong Kong. The kids there were rough-hewn but playful, each of them seemed to be a crude ore that needed to be refined. Once an impatient kid asked her a question during a lesson: Why did they have to learn art and what was it? She thought for a while about this important issue, then replied: Art enriches life, and art itself is a wonder. Wherever you feel harmony, there art is. She thus gave the class an example that there was an old couple in their late seventies strolling happily along the island's harbour at least twice a week in the morning. She saw wonder in that couple. She then encouraged her students to discover art around them.

It has been ten years since she left the school, she wishes she could have the chance to tell them that she sees wonder in Chinese words.

325

Special thanks to my husband, Hung Tat Leung, for his enormous support, and to my friend, Mr. Paul Grover, for his patience in answering my numerous English questions in writing this book.